The Fiction
of
Rohinton Mistry

The Fiction
of
Rohinton Mistry

critical studies

Edited by
Jaydipsinh Dodiya

PRESTIGE

Published by
Prestige Books
3/28, East Patel Nagar
New Delhi 110 008

ISBN: 81-7551-046-3

1998

Photo Typesetting by
Pivot Computers
Delhi 110 006
Ph. 98110-35585

Printed at
Chaman Offset Printers
New Delhi 110 002

Contents

Preface
9

Indian-Canadian Writing

Literature of the Indian Diaspora in Canada
Jaydipsinh Dodiya
11

**Fiction across Worlds: Some Writers of
Indian Origin in Canada**
M.L. Pandit
14

**"When Old Tracks are Lost" :
Rohinton Mistry's Fiction as Diasporic Discourse**
Nilufer E. Bharucha
23

Comparative Studies

**Parsi Culture and Vision in
Rohinton Mistry's *Such a Long Journey* and
Firdaus Kanga's *Trying to Grow***
N.P. Sharma
32

**Modes of Resistance in the South-Asian Novel:
A Study of the Fiction by Bapsi Sidhwa,
Rohinton Mistry and Yasmine Gooneratne**
Gita Viswanath
38

**From behind a Fine Veil: A Feminist Reading
of Three Parsi Novels**
Nilufer E. Bharucha
44

Tales from Firozsha Baag

Local Colour in *Tales from Firozsha Baag*
S. Ramaswamy
54

**Geophysical Imagination and History in the
Fiction of Rohinton Mistry and Bharati Mukherjee**
Neelam Tikkha
61

Bad Faith in "Lend Me Your Light"
Subhash Chandra
66

Such a Long Journey

***Such a Long Journey*: A Critical Study**
Jaydipsinh Dodiya
70

***Such a Long Journey* and Its Critical Acclaim**
M. Mani Meitei
73

Thematic Concerns in *Such a Long Journey*
Anita Myles
85

The Parsi Community in *Such a Long Journey*
Jaydipsinh Dodiya
93

A Fine Balance

Novel as History: A Study of
Such a Long Journey and *A Fine Balance*
Nila Shah
96

"And everything ends badly": A Reading of *A Fine Balance*
Vinita Dhondiyal Bhatnagar
102

Designer Quilt: A Study of *A Fine Balance*
B. Indira
110

A Critical Appraisal of *A Fine Balance*
Nila Shah
115

The Text of Cruelty:
Power and Violence in *A Fine Balance*
Pramod K. Nayar
119

The Politics of Survival and Domination in *A Fine Balance*
Novy Kapadia
127

Index
135

Contributors

Nilufer E. Bharucha, University of Bombay

Vinita Dhondiyal Bhatnagar, CIEFL, Lucknow

Subhash Chandra, S.B.S. College, University of Delhi

Jaydipsinh Dodiya, Shardagram Arts & Comm. College, Mangrol

B. Indira, Andhra University, Visakhapatnam

Novy Kapadia, S.G.T.B. Khalsa College, University of Delhi

M. Mani Meitei, Manipur University, Imphal

Anita Myles, University of Gorakhpur

Pramod K. Nayar, Kuvempu University, Shimoga

M.L. Pandit, IGNOU, New Delhi

S. Ramaswamy, Bangalore University

Nila Shah, Jasani Arts and Commerce College, Rajkot

N.P. Sharma, Govt. P.G. College, Dhar

Neelam Tikkha, Kamla Nehru College of Engg., Nagpur

Gita Viswanath, Tolani Arts College, Adipur

Preface

Perhaps the most interesting aspect of the fiction at the turn of the present century, from the Indian point of view, is the emergence of new talent. A number of novelists have produced significant novels, making a mark in the literary world. The most sensational literary event in the recent past was, probably, the publication of Salman Rushdie's magnum opus *Midnight's Children* which became an international success instantly on its release. It created a generation of young Indian novelists who eagerly followed his footsteps. Among these novelists, the notable ones are: Vikram Seth, Amitav Ghosh, Upamanyu Chatterjee, Shashi Tharoor, Mukul Kesavan and Rohinton Mistry.

Rohinton Mistry, the socio-political novelist, has emerged as a significant literary figure during the recent years. It is interesting to scrutinize his publishing career. His maiden anthology of short stories *Tales from Firozsha Baag* (1987) was followed by a remarkable first novel *Such a Long Journey* (1991) which received a wide acclaim the world over. Four years after *Such a Long Journey,* Mistry published *A Fine Balance* which has been hailed as a landmark in the history of Indian fiction as also in Indian-Canadian writing. It is a novel that wafts the enchanted reader across vast seas of experience, from the ecstasy of the Indian Independence in 1947, to its traumatic Emergency under Indira Gandhi's regime in 1975. Though Mistry has published only three works to-date—a story collection and two novels—he has gained immense popularity as a literary figure. Like Rushdie, another expatriate Indian writer, Mistry has achieved phenomenal success and received several prestigious awards. It will therefore indeed be rewarding to study his works in detail and evaluate his contribution to contemporary writing.

I cannot close these prefatory remarks without thanking those who helped me in the preparation of this volume. I express my gratitude to Dr. A.K. Singh, Head of the Department of English, Saurashtra University, Rajkot, for inspiring me to take up this project; to Professor I.G. Purohit of BRS College, Mangrol, for his help

and guidance; to all the contributors for their scholarly papers; to Dr.
R.K. Dhawan for editorial help; and to my brother Mr. K.K. Dodiya
who has been a constant source of inspiration. Finally, I put on record
my sincere thanks to Prestige Books for bringing out this book most ex-
peditiously and elegantly.

                                                JAYDIPSINH DODIYA

Literature of the Indian Diaspora in Canada

JAYDIPSINH DODIYA

Literature is fundamentally an expression of life through the medium of language. It is the criticism of life. It reflects the social surroundings of the writer's time. It is also the mirror of the society. In this paper I am going to talk about the Indian writers who have migrated to Canada; their literary creation can be called 'Literature of the Indian Diaspora in Canada.'

Indian-Canadian literature as an identifiable body came into existence around the 1970s. A recent study by Suguna Siri (1988) records that between 1962 and 1982, a surprisingly large number of South-Asian writers in English published their work. There were about one hundred and two writers who published one hundred and ninety six works in more than one genre. During the last decade there has been an equal number of publications. Suguna Siri applies the term South-Asian to those Canadians who trace their origins from one of the following South-Asian countries: India, Sri Lanka, Pakistan and Bangladesh. It also includes the writers who came directly to Canada from one of the South-Asian countries or who came indirectly by way of Britain or other erstwhile British colonies such as South Africa, East Africa or the Caribbean and the Pacific islands, if we talk more pragmatically about Canadian Islands.

There were two very distinct waves of immigrants from South-Asia: the first wave of immigration occurred during the British Raj and the other after independence. The literature produced by the writers during these two distinct chronological phases have their own distinct stages of development as well as their period of growth and gestation. The first wave of immigrants came in the latter half of the nineteenth century. It consisted of indentured labourers from Indian sub-continents who filled up the gap created by the abolition of slavery. These immigrants were mostly illiterate and whatever literature they gave or created, was oral. The real Indian-Canadian South-Asian writers during the second phase of immigration consisted of traders who came to Canada to provide basic cultural and business service to the earlier groups and who earned their living from serving their own countrymen in Canada. Of course there was not much literary activity even during this phase. Moyez Vassanji (from East Africa) has given an authentic documentary of the Indian Diaspora in East Africa in his brilliant novel[1] *The Gunny Sack* (1989). In this novel he traces the history of the Gujaratis (Ismaili Khoja in particular) in Zanzibar and Dar-es-salam from 1885 to 1970. The people with a higher level of education or business expertise struck their roots in their adopted homeland and provided a richer soil for literary growth. This second wave of immigration started in the early fifties. Educated South-Asians of newly independent countries set out to try their fortune in Canada and other European or American countries with sufficient brain-power to be used for developing technology. The decade that followed may be called the gold-rush period of the second wave as very highly qualified South-Asians ventured into the overseas countries of the western world. The period of the seventies was a decade of reaction. Non-South-Asian segment of population started being conscious of the South-Asian influx and reacted against it in varying degrees. The idea of racism did not exist so far, or if it did exist, it was well controlled. But during this period the opposition of the indigenous population grew and brought about a situation in which the immigrant South-Asians were subjected to persecution and insult as well as injustice simply on racist grounds. The literature produced during this phase reflects the reactionary opposition of the indigenous people and the consequent suffering, indignity and injustice undergone by the immigrants.

The first South-Asian immigrants entered Canada in the 1890s. They were mostly persons belonging to Sikh regiments passing through Canada in 1897 after attending Queen Victoria's Diamond Jubilee Celebration. By the year 1907, there were approximately two thousand Indians in British Columbia including about 700 who had been expelled from Washington state earlier that year. In September 1907, a large segment of the white population of that province numbering about two hundred thousand made a massive attack on the Asians, consisting of fifteen thousand Chinese and Japanese and two thousand Indians. This opposition and reaction on the part of the white population laid to the passage of 'orders-in-councils' in 1910 that effectively controlled the Asian immigration. By these orders each immigrant was required to pay two hundred dollars as head-tax.

And again, it was necessary for them to have a continuous passage from the homeland. The latter condition restricted and precluded Indians from entering Canada. Naturally the volume of immigration was very thin and the number of the Indians who entered Canada were only in two figures year after year. There was an increasing opposition and prejudice amongst white population. It was during this period that the worst racist incidents such as Koma Gata Maru happened. The Koma Gata Maru was a Japanese ship chartered by Gurdeep Singh and had 376 persons as passengers. Gurdeep Singh had also negotiated with a Hongkong merchant who would purchase the Canadian Lumber which the ship would carry on its return voyage. The Koma Gata Maru reached Vancouver harbour on May 23, 1914. For two months, the ship and its passengers were quarantined off the coast while the Government, under Governor General Lord Grey and Prime Minister Wilfrid Laurier, discussed how to get rid of the "Brown Peril," and then the ship was sent back. Only a few passengers, who were returning immigrants and therefore could not be refused entry, were admitted.

Rohinton Mistry and Bharati Mukherjee are well-known immigrant Canadian writers whose literary creation makes our concept of Literature of the Indian Diaspora in Canada quite clear.

Fiction across Worlds: Some Writers of Indian Origin in Canada

M.L. PANDIT

T he Commonwealth is a brotherhood of states spread over all the five continents of the world. The nations that form parts of it have much more in common than only the English language. The Commonwealth countries share areas of creative interest that are often missing in other federations based on common geographical, economic or political considerations. The Canadian nation consists of a multiplicity of races and cultures that is rarely encountered outside the Commonwealth. From time to time, through accidents of history, a variety of people of different races, backgrounds and cultures have sought refuge in this country of the English and French speaking peoples. Multiculturalism is an essential aspect of the Canadian scene, and it is reflected in the works of the writers of this land. It should come as no surprise that their imagination leaps across worlds in search of suitable themes and motifs for creative writing.

There is a great variety in the Canadian immigrant experience as recorded in literature. During the last fifty years, many writers of Indian origin, once or twice removed from their first homeland, have gone as immigrants to Canada. One of the foremost among them was Bharati Mukherjee—now in the USA—who could boast of a triple inheritance from her Bengali Indian antecedents to the years spent in an American university and to the subsequent experience of living and teaching in Canada. In works like *Wife* (1976) and *Jasmine* (1990) she provides a realistic account of the pressures facing an Indian woman in a male-dominated North American society. In collaboration with Clark Blaise, her American-born husband, Bharati Mukherjee wrote a dual autobiography, *Days and Nights in Calcutta* (1977). It is an account of a year they spent together in India. She went to revisit a world she had left, he to explore a world he had married into. The contrast between the two parts of the book stresses the difference in their points of view. Clark

Blaise sees the richness of India and the strangeness of his experience. He faithfully records the events of their journey together, as any other foreign tourist would do. Bharati Mukherjee, on the other hand, with her knowledge of Bengali, hears gossip, pain, pressure and privilege of the people she encounters. The same episodes carry different overtones in the two separate accounts. It is the difference between an outsider's and an insider's view. With the publication of the book back in the West, it highlights the contrast between a native and a foreign writer.

The immigrant writer's contribution is best illustrated by a short story, which comes at the end of *The Middleman and Other Stories* (1988), a book of Bharati Mukherjee dealing entirely with the immigrant experience. Entitled "The Management of Grief," it is a fictional account of some Canadians of Indian origin, who have lost their close relatives in the Air India jumbo jet disaster off the coast of Ireland. It is significant that the flight originated in Canada, and was on its way to India. The majority of the travellers were Indians. Being an Indian-born herself, Bharati Mukherjee expresses the sense of grief of those left behind in Canada more authentically than any native Canadian, American or British writer could. The outlook of one of the characters in the story is pointedly Indian: "Kusum says we can't escape our fate. She says that all those people—our husbands, my boys, her girl with the nightingale voice, all those Hindus, Christians, Sikhs, Muslims, Parsis, and atheists on that plane—were fated to die together off this beautiful bay."[1] Again, note what the narrator, Shaila Bhave, says: "I am trapped between two modes of knowledge. At thirty-six I am too old to start over and too young to give up. Like my husband's spirit, I flutter between worlds." (189)

Another Mukherjee character, Panna Patel, in "A Wife's Story" complains, "In my red silk sari I'm conspicuous." (25) This is a conclusion corroborated by Meera Shastri, an Indian immigrant in Canada, in her essay, "Canadian Experience": "Within a week of my arrival in Toronto, I realized that the sari was not a practical outfit for the Canadian winter and took to wearing pants. It was just a short while before I began to feel self-conscious about wearing saris even when the weather was good."[2] Numerous similar observations are reflected in the experiences and writings of Canadian writers of fiction of Indian origin.

Neil Bissoondath, V.S. Naipaul's sister's son, is a West Indian of the East Indian origin. He was born in Trinidad and went in 1973 to Toronto to complete a degree in French at the York University. He stayed on to live and write in Canada. For obvious reasons, his fiction carries the triple flavour of his diverse backgrounds. *Digging up the*

Mountains (1985) is a collection of short stories in which he examines the intellectual implications of the motifs of changing places and ex-changing cultures. This reminds one of the manner in which Naipaul tackles these themes in some of his early fictional works dealing with the life of the East Indian immigrants in Trinidad. In one of his essays, Bissoondath refers to the Canadian oil company executive, who was looking for an apartment in Toronto. This man rejected buildings with East Indian tenants because he believed that cockroaches were symbols of good luck in their culture. Such misunderstandings persist and give us some idea of what an author is up against while transforming immi-grant experience into fiction.

Nazneen Sadiq was born in Kashmir in 1944. She went to Canada when she was twenty, and stayed on to write fiction that has the flavour of her immigrant experience. Her *Ice Bangles* (1988) is a collection of short stories. In the title story, Naila, the narrator, living in Canada, goes home to attend the wedding of her brother. It comes as a surprise to her that her brother's bride, though quite charming, is dark-skinned. Her comment in this regard is revealing: "The fair-skinned northerners had practised for centuries the same discrimination which their British masters had been accused of. Her mother, who had hoped secretly for a Kashmiri wife for her only son, had been cheated." (*Between Worlds,* 31) When Naila notices the children of the domestic servants peeping over the boundary walls at the glittering festivities, "She was conscious for the first time of social divisions and found them disturbing. Five years of living in Canada had awakened a social conscience which emerged with the embarrassment of adolescent acne." (34)

So far I have referred to three writers of fiction, who coming with their Indian and other backgrounds, write about the immigrant experi-ence in Canada, drawing very much on their first hand experience. They highlight the problems of immigrants confronted with the situation of living in the midst of an alien culture. It creates more problems for them when they go back, even though temporarily, to the places of their birth. Now I would like to draw your attention to a Canadian writer of Indian origin, who, while living in his adopted home, writes most authentically about his experience in India before going to Canada.

Rohinton Mistry, a Parsi, was born in Bombay in 1952, and emi-grated to Canada in 1975. For ten years, he worked in a bank, studying English and philosophy part time at the University of Toronto. His first short story fetched him a Hart House Prize for fiction in 1983. His sto-ries have been published in major Canadian literary journals and an-thologies. His three works of fiction, *Tales from Firozsha Baag* (1987),

Such a Long Journey (1991) and *A Fine Balance* (1995) are widely acclaimed to the extent of the last named work being nominated for the Booker Award 1996. That he did not finally get the award is as much a comment on the system of selection as on the quality of the other novels that figured in the final judgement. It is a case similar to that of V.S. Naipaul, that great West Indian writer of the second half of the twentieth century, being nominated for the Nobel Prize but not getting it though some writers of lesser merit have secured the award. Boris Pasternak, the Russian dissident writer with just one *Doctor Zhivago* to boast of, would be a case in point.

Such a Long Journey (1991) is a brilliant first novel by one of the most remarkable writers of fiction to have emerged from India in recent years. It is set in Bombay against the backdrop of the Indo-Pakistan war of 1971 and the emergence of Bangladesh as a separate independent nation. The novel tells the story of a Parsi bank official, Gustad Noble, and the peculiar way in which the conflict in the Indian sub-continent affects him and his family.

The remarkable thing about *Such a Long Journey* is its absolute Indianness, without any trace of the Canadian immigrant experience that the author must have gone through for fifteen years before the publication of the book. It is steeped in the atmosphere of Bombay, particularly of the exclusive Parsi community of that city. The Khodadad Building, an apartment house, where Gustad Noble lives along with his Parsi neighbours, is a world in itself. Dilnavaz, his wife is beset by the usual Indian superstitions, encouraged by Miss Kutpitia, the mysterious spinster. When Sohrab, the elder son of Gustad, refuses to join the IIT, against the wishes of his father, and leaves home, Dilnavaz circles a lemon over his head, offering the juice of it in a sweetened drink to the half-wit, Tehmul-Lungraa. For general good luck, she hangs a lemon and some green chillies on a string above the front door from inside. Again, she consults Miss Kutpitia, when baffled by the prolonged illness of her daughter, Roshan, in order to devise ways of warding off the evil eye. The world of Indian superstition in *Such a Long Journey* is far removed from the western society of Toronto in Canada, where Rohinton Mistry wrote the novel.

Mistry shows an Indian's knowledge about corruption being an ingrained part of life at all levels in India. He reiterates how an ordinary citizen can get nothing done without bribes, if he has any dealings with the municipality, the police department or the politicians. Dr. Paymaster, the family physician of Gustad Noble, points out: "that municipal corruption was only a microcosmic manifestation of the greed, dishonesty, and moral turpitude that flourished at the country's centre. He described meticulously how, from the very top, whence all power flowed, there also dripped the pus of putrefaction, inflicting every stratum of society below."[3]

Mistry reminds us how goods donated by people to support the war effort at the time of the Chinese invasion later turned up for sale in the Chor Bazaar. He makes critical references to Indira Gandhi's handling of the Bangladesh War. The episode of Nagarwala cheating the State Bank of India of several lakhs of rupees, by impersonating the Prime Minister on the phone, is woven into the fabric of the novel and intermingled with the fate of Major Bilimoria, a friend of Gustad Noble. A notable concern in *Such a Long Journey* is the raw deal that Bilimoria gets from the Government out of working for the RAW. Gustad gets involved in the shady deal and draws his friend, Dinshawji, too into it. The death of Dinshawji from cancer is a high point in the novel, as it reveals the truly noble side of Gustad, who is the sole male mourner at the Parsi funeral rites that follow. It is a kind of cleansing process that pushes Gustad very close to an intense spiritual experience.

Gustad's dream of launching his son as a successful engineer is a lofty one, and a purely Indian one at that. "The dream of IIT took shape, then took hold of their imaginations. And the Indian Institute of Technology became the promised land. It was El Dorado and Camelot, it was Xanadu and Oz. It was the home of the Holy Grail." (66) One cannot fail to appreciate the tongue-in-cheek flavour of this passage.

To his young daughter's question, "Daddy, why is West Pakistan killing the people in East Pakistan?" (81) Gustad can offer only this simplistic answer: "East Pakistan is poor, they said to West, we are always hungry, please give us a fair share. But West said no. Then East said, in that case we don't want to work with you. So, as punishment, West Pakistan is killing and burning East Pakistan." (81) That is as close a summation of the political upheaval as any.

Peerbhoy Paanwala in *Such a Long Journey* is an institution by himself. He has a *paan* for all seasons, but the one most in demand is the bed-breaker or *palungtode paan* with its renowned aphrodisiacal properties. Possessing a rich faculty for myth-making, Peerbhoy suggests that even the Moghul emperors used this variety of *paan* when they went to their harems. To young boys, he would offer a *paan* which would cleanse their heads of boyish impurities and help them concentrate on their studies. When the Bangladesh war is at its apex, Peerbhoy rises to great heights in weaving a myth about the doings of Gen. Yahya Khan and his military governor of East Pakistan.

Gustad Noble's dreams and expectations are modest indeed, but circumstances prevailing in the India of his times conspire to deny him
even these. It is very hard on him that he cannot make things happen in
such a way as to fulfil his aspirations. Forces, stranger than himself,
come in the way of his achieving his ambitions. His elder son does not
join the IIT; Roshan, his favourite child, suffers from a prolonged illness; Dinshawji, his best friend, dies of cancer; and another friend, Bilimoria, betrays his trust. Gradually, Gustad Noble modifies his dreams
and dilutes his expectations. It is quite obvious that he is not in control
of things. But this does not make him turn into a defeatist. In the true
oriental way, his triumph consists in the calm manner with which he
faces each trial of his life. It lies in his acceptance of the harsh realities
of the world to which he belongs. His grandest moment comes towards
the end of the novel, when he forgives his erring son, and clasps him to
his bosom in a noble gesture of acceptance of Sohrab's decision to lead
his own life.

Four years after *Such a Long Journey,* Mistry published *A Fine Balance*.[4] It took him that long time to ruminate over the gestation of an
epic of a novel stretched over 752 pages. One would like to think that he
was not inspired by the success of Vikram Seth's monumental work, *A
Suitable Boy* which is more than a match for the great Victorian novels
of Dickens and Thackeray, at least in its awesome length. As far as the
title of Mistry's novel goes, the book does maintain a 'fine balance'
among the multitude of characters and the various strands of the complex plot that it projects. It draws hugely upon the traditional art of the
Indian narrative fiction as one comes across in the Sanskrit *Katha Sarit
Sagar*, the virtual ocean of stories from Kashmir. The manner in which
the characters and events are introduced, and then skilfully linked together to run into a stream of stories as in Boccacio's *De Cameron* and
Chaucer's *Canterbury Tales*, not to mention our own *Panchtantra* and
Hitopadesha or the Arabian Nights from the Middle East. Mistry's own
cherished metropolis, Bombay, 'the city by the sea,' leads the reader to
a 'village by the river' up in the mountains, and takes him back on a
picaresque journey of discovery to the same cosmopolitan city of multiple dimensions. *A Fine Balance* is a novel that wafts the enchanted
reader across vast seas of experience, from the ecstasy of the Indian Independence, in 1947, to its traumatic Emergency under Indira Gandhi's
Congress rule, in 1975. The immensity of the contrast is highlighted by
Mistry in his inimitable forthright Indian English presentation of facts
with a touch of his irony and humour. The jokes and puns and the topi-
cal references are all Indian, going beyond the narrow Parsi circle—

Mistry's favourite ground from his very first work of fiction onwards—
into the much vaster caste-ridden Hindu society.

It is possible only in India that Mistry's Ishvar or Narayan, cobblers
by caste and profession could be the cause of an upheaval in their village by deliberately changing their trade to tailoring. It would seem un-
believable to the readers of Rohinton Mistry outside India, but that's
how it happens in our caste-ridden land as all Indians of various hues
and colours know to their discomfiture. Mistry comments on this dismal
situation by a straightforward narration of events rather than a philo-
sophic reflection in depth. After all, he is a story-teller par excellence,
and knows his craft well. His method is more effective in highlighting
the differences in castes than if he were to write a discursive critique on
the much maligned theme. After all, what could be more touching to
heart than Roopa, the self-obliterating mother of Ishvar and Narayan,
losing the chastity of her mango-like breasts and the rest of her charming young body to the lascivious watchman of the rich man's orchard in
exchange for a few oranges she covets for her sons. (120) The entire
prurient episode is Mistry's harsh comment on the exploitation of low-
caste women who willy-nilly have to succumb to the machinations of
their very upper-caste male seducers. From Rohinton Mistry's fictional
account, so graphically presented, one gets an idea that this is the reality
that still repeats itself in the Indian sub-continent. The tragic irony is
that a high-caste lust-perverted man who is likely to be polluted even by
the shadow of a low-caste, still covets and sleeps with impunity with a
desirable *Chamaran* (woman of the cobbler class). This anamoly of
double-standards has been equally interestingly projected by Mulk Raj
Anand in Untouchable. Hence, it remains a debatable point what is right
and what is wrong in a dubious social context, and Mistry is acutely
aware of this great divide. What is more, he focuses our attention on this
irrational travesty of justice in Independent India. He lays stress on the
secular character of the Indian ethos by demonstrating how Hindu
Dukhi's sons and Muslim Ashraf's family look after each other in times
of uncertainty and communal discord, and so cement bonds of unity for
all times to come in spite of the British strategy of dividing the country
into India and Pakistan.

The value of *A Fine Balance* as a fictional account of historical
facts is enhanced by the Indian Parsi writer's intimate critical knowledge of the events of history and social background that provides the
canvas to his novel. It needs an Indian-born and Indian-bred writer to
appreciate and evaluate the current situation in India from a sympathetic
as well as critical point of view at any given period of time. His account

of the Bombay Parsi community and its travails—the favourite subject of Mistry's Canadian-Indian fiction in English—on which he concentrates in all the three fictional works of his is here projected through the life and experiences of Dina, who is unfortunately left to fend for herself after the death of her loving husband, Rustom, in a freak accident. Dina is a symbol of rebellion against the time-worn social and religious traditions of her exclusive community. Hence, it is only appropriate that on her should fall the onus of helping out by way of providing steady work to the cobbler turned tailors, Ishvar and Omprakash, and Maneck, the son of her former schoolmate, whom she is constrained to accept as a clandestine paying guest.

Dina's rebellion against the tyranny of her autocratic brother and the traditionally accepted norms of her orthodox Parsi community reflects the change from the old to the new ways of thinking in Bombay and India. The detailed account of the Parsi rites and rituals, and family relationships is a world of authentic ethnic revelations that one normally expects from a social historian or anthropologist. But Mistry provides these elements as the sauce to his main dish of India under Indira's Emergency in *A Fine Balance*. At the same time, the tragedy of life that pursues Dina from childhood, through school days, to adulthood and marital bliss with the consequent loss of a joyous anchor in life, are a lesson in the divergence between one's ambitious dreams and their elusive fruition. Mistry's powerful novel makes a brave attempt to achieve a fine balance between the heavy odds pitted against the fragility of life and the ruthlessness of actual happenings at a troubled time in recent Indian history, when the Emergency encouraged some politicians to check the rampant high birth rate by forced and unethical vasectomy and other cruel methods. It is remarkable that Rohinton Mistry has written a popular novel based on such a controversial theme, and that the end product was short-listed for a Booker Award.

The conclusion that I would like to draw in this brief essay relates to the various ways in which the immigrant writers of Indian origin in Canada convert their experience into fiction. Few among them would opt to project their newly acquired western values, which perhaps they fail to appreciate fully. Some, like Bharati Mukherjee and Nazneen Sadiq, concentrate on the changes in the attitudes and sensibility of their fictional characters, when confronted with the dilemmas of cross-cultural concerns. This is, no doubt, a rewarding way of projecting the Indian immigrant experience in Canada. But we should not under-estimate the contribution of writers of fiction like Rohinton Mistry, who open a window on India for their Canadian and other western readers. *Such a*

Long Journey tells us more about the Parsi community in Bombay than a book of sociology possibly could. What is more, Mistry is able to project the emotional life and personal relationships of the Parsis as a valuable part of the wider human experience at the international level by writing about these things from across the worlds. The Indian readers of Mistry will react to this book in their own way. For them, he presents an interesting slice of their own life, which for them is a most valued thing. While Salman Rushdie, another Indian expatriate writer, offends with his satiric denunciations, Rohinton Mistry entertains while he exposes the frailties of his characters with his gentle humour and an eye for the comic in human nature.

NOTES

1. Bharati Mukherjee, *The Middleman and Other Stories* (Penguin Books India, 1990), p. 184.
2. Milly Charon, ed., *Between Two Worlds: The Canadian Immigrant Experience* (Montreal: Nu-Age Editions, 1988), p. 284.
3. Rohinton Mistry, *Such a Long Journey* (London: Faber and Faber, 1991), pp. 312-13.
4. Rohinton Mistry, *A Fine Balance* (London: Faber and Faber, 1996).

"When Old Tracks are Lost": Rohinton Mistry's Fiction as Diasporic Discourse

NILUFER E. BHARUCHA

As an Indian who now lives in and writes from Canada, Rohinton Mistry is a writer of the Indian Diaspora. However, Mistry is also a Parsi Zoroastrian and as a person whose ancestors were forced into exile by the Islamic conquest of Iran,[1] he was in Diaspora even in India. Like other Parsi writers,[2] his writing is informed by this experience of double displacement.

Within its broad frame, Indian Diaspora is a historical and economic phenomenon which can be divided into four distinct phases. The first is set in the colonial period when Indians were transported as indentured labourers to Britain's African and West Indian colonies. The second phase can be contextualized within the immediate postcolonial times when Indians went to Britain and Canada to supplement the West's war-depleted work force. In the third phase, students from India went to universities in the West, mainly in the USA, and rarely if ever returned. Finally, there is the Petroleum Diaspora, in which Indians went to the oil-producing countries of the Middle East in search of "Petrodollars." These Diasporas which began towards the middle of the last century are now nearly a hundred and fifty years old.

Indians of almost all these Diasporas have sought to record the manner in which they have adapted to their new environment and how they have experienced both identification with and alienation from their old and new homelands.[3] The bonding of culture, religion, literature and language is especially strong in a Diasporic situation but where it provides ethnic identity and a sense of self, it can also alienate from the host culture. It is this displacement which gives Diasporic writing its peculiar qualities of loss and nostalgia. The world view provided by such writers is thus a fragmented one—whether they write of their new homelands or their old. As Rushdie has said in *Imaginary Homelands*, they are obliged to "deal in broken mirrors some of whose fragments have been lost."[4]

As a Parsi, Mistry is in yet another Diaspora—a much older one. In pre-colonial India Parsis were allowed to practise their ancient monotheistic religion but there was a price to pay for this freedom. They could not proselytize and had to adopt the costumes, traditions and language of their Hindu hosts.[5] Their religious festivals had to be kept low-key and above all they could not bear arms. These unequal conditions provided fertile ground for the development of feelings of alienation from India. In colonial times, the Parsis enjoyed a privileged status as brokers between the British and other Indians. They became very Westernized and identified almost completely with the colonial masters. This in turn has created problems in postcolonial India where their social and economic status has been much downgraded, prompting many Parsis to move to the West and shed their Indian identities. This too has resulted in psychological trauma as, in the West, they have been lumped together with other Asian groups—specifically Indians.

Writing done by Parsis has borne witness to these old and new travails experienced by their co-religionists. The pre-colonial oral tradition of the Gujarati folk song—*Garba*—records the arrival of the first band of Parsis to India and the conditions upon which they were given refuge. The Persian text, *Kissah Sanjan*, by Kaikobad Sanjana in 1600 CE, tells the same story, but in the written tradition. Both these texts also valorize the glorious Persian past, i.e. the Persian Empire, recall Iranian heroes and detail the life of the Prophet Zoroaster and his monotheistic, this-worldly religion. Colonial Parsi writers like Behram Malbari and Cornelia Sorabji also displayed diasporic traits of nostalgia and loss in their poetry, sketches, fiction and autobiographical work.[6] There isn't much Parsi writing available in either the nationalist phase or in the immediate postcolonial times. This was the period when, under the guidance of Gandhi and Nehru, a distinct, composite Indian identity was being forged. The majority of Parsis, however, did not stake a claim to this identity and in spite of the exhortations of nationalist Parsis like Dadabhoy Naoroji and Phirozsha Mehta, they remained aloof as India gained independence from Britain and then went through the holocaust of Partition. However, starting with the 1980s, the Parsi voice has been heard once again.

The 1980s also saw the emergence of the second generation of postcolonial Indian English writers. This period coincides with what Edward Said has called the second stage of anti-colonial resistance, when a postcolonial society, having achieved political sovereignty, makes a determined effort to shake off the continuing socio-cultural domination of the erstwhile colonizer—the battle now is for "cultural territory."[7] As

Rushdie has put it, postcolonial society then seeks to "repossess its own history."[8] Frantz Fanon has called this the "Cultural Nationalist" phase.[9]

In the case of Parsi writers, to the postcolonial concerns of cultural autonomy and repossession of history was added the need to assert a distinct identity and recall the ethno-religious characteristics of Parsis. As the end of the twentieth century approaches, the Parsis are in demographic decline. A ban on conversions, late marriages, a low birth rate, marriages outside the fold by Parsi women whose offspring is then not accepted as Parsis, has led to a situation where only around a 100,000 Parsis survive world-wide today. So in a way, Parsi writers today are trying to record for posterity the story of the Parsi race and their ancient Zoroastrian faith. In an interview, Rohinton Mistry has said that when the Parsis have disappeared from the face of the earth, his writing will "preserve a record of how they lived, to some extent."[10] However, he claims that this is not the central focus of his writing.

In spite of this disclaimer, Mistry's discourse does revolve around the detailing of Parsi identity. It also reveals how Parsis are learning to cope with the reality of postcolonial India and how they are coming to terms with their new lives in the West. In common with other postcolonial writing, Mistry's fiction is fashioned in the form of alternative narratives and employs anti-realist modes of narration. This not only challenges elitist Master Narratives but privileges the marginal and provides resistance to Western hegemony.

However, this is not all that Mistry's discourse does. As a Parsi he is on the periphery even in India, so his discourse also challenges and resists the totalization of the dominant culture within India itself. Mistry has also experimented with linguistic hybridity and celebrated the unique Parsi idiom in his writing. This is true of both *Tales from Firozsha Baag* and *Such a Long Journey*.[11]

In *Tales from Firozsha Baag*, Mistry presents his readers with ghetto-like Parsi world, where the postcolonial Indian reality is firmly shut out and where the residents display a siege-mentality. In these short stories, Mistry grapples with what Kulke has called identity-forming elements of Parsiness—the Zoroastrian faith, a shared history of flight from Iran and refuge in India, a colonial elite consciousness and feeling of unease in decolonized India.[12] In this insular world, the protagonists' lives revolve around the Parsi housing complex of Firozsha Baag, the Zoroastrian religion, the Fire-temple, the Parsi priests, the Parsi calendar, Parsi cuisine. This discourse also highlights Parsi idiosyncrasies and bloody-mindedness. Among Indians, Parsis have a not undeserved

reputation for eccentricity and even testiness. This was tolerated in colonial India, where thanks to their proximity to the colonizers, the Parsis
had a certain license and were almost treated like honorary *sahibs*. However, in postcolonial India the Parsis have to contend with a downgraded
status and there is little sympathy for their fads and foibles and above
all their haughtiness *vis a vis* other Indians.

This is nowhere clearer than in the first story from Mistry's collection—"Auspicious Occasion." Here the *Bawaji* (an affectionate/pejora-
tive term for a Parsi male), Rustomji, is as eccentric and bloody-minded
as a Parsi can possibly get. His wife, Mehroo, is pious and given to
much praying and *agiary*-going.[13] India is firmly kept out of their Parsi
world and about the only contact they have with non-Parsis is through
their servants. Rustomji covertly lusts after his cleaning lady—always
called Ganga by Parsis, irrespective of her actual name. This is yet another commonplace characteristic of the *Bawaji*. In fact, both Rustomji
and Mehroo are almost stereotypical Parsis and what saves them and the
story from becoming banal is Mistry's deft introduction of two incidents—one where Rustomji is spat upon by a *paan*-chewer and the second where Mehroo is shocked by the murder of the Parsi priest, the *das-
toorji*. These events clearly indicate the sense of unease Parsis experience in postcolonial India. Rustomji's elite-consciousness suffers a se-
vere denting when a *ghaati*[14] lets loose a stream of *paan*-spittle on him,
soiling his crisp white coat, the *dagli*. This wasn't done deliberately but
Rustomji takes it as a personal slight. His self-esteem is further dam-
aged when instead of being intimidated by his ravings and rantings, the
ghaatis get together and almost beat him up. He escapes only by playing
the clown—"his desperate search for a way out was rewarded—a sudden inspiration which just might work. He reached his fingers into his
mouth, dislodged the dentures, and spat them out onto his palm. . . . The
collapsed mouth and flapping lips appeased everyone. A general titter-
ing spread through the assembly. Rustomji the clown was triumphant."
(18) This is a sad but true reflection of how Parsi image has been downgraded in decolonized India. At another level, his wife Mehroo is confronted with the disintegration of yet another aspect of Parsi identity—
its essential sameness. She is shocked that the Parsi priest has been murdered by his own Parsi servant. This threatens the support-system, the
closing-of-ranks syndrome, which has helped preserve the Parsi identity
for over a thousand years even in the all-embracing, all-encompassing
ethos of Hinduism.

This near-total alienation from postcolonial India has pushed more
and more Parsis into a Western Diaspora. This is evident in the story

"Lend Me Your Light." What is of importance here is the feeling of guilt connected with this voluntary exodus. The enforced Diaspora from Iran had engendered a feeling of self-esteem, as the Parsis had gone into exile to preserve their religion and their way of life. The protagonist of this story says, "I'm guilty of the sin of hubris for seeking emigration out of the land of my birth and paying the price in burnt out eyes: I, Tiresias, blind and throbbing between two lives, the one in Bombay and the one to come in Toronto." (180) This story also presents the Parsis who have totally identified themselves with postcolonial India. Such Parsis are in a minority and generally frowned upon by their co-religionists. The narrator's brother Percy is such a man. He is actively involved in work at grass-roots level in a village and feels little kinship with his family and even less with his childhood friend Jamshed, who is totally Westernized and now lives in New York.

The last story in this collection, "Swimming Lessons," is the only one set fully in Canada. However, even here the Canadian world is juxtaposed with Indian memories. The distinctness of Parsi identity here is not overtly invoked but this does not necessarily mean Canada is now home. The initial failure of the protagonist to master the Chowpatty waters in Bombay, as well as the swimming pool water in Canada, symbolizes his failure to assimilate in either society. However, by the end of the story, water, the amniotic fluid, is the medium through which he is reborn. He reopens his eyes under water in his bath-tub and sees life in dual perspective—what Rushdie has called "stereoscopic vision"—both Eastern and Western.

Mistry's first novel, *Such a Long Journey*, returns to Bombay and the Parsi world. Even more than the short stories, this novel is Diasporic discourse. Here Mistry has very overtly attempted to deconstruct and repossess his past. He was born in 1952 and left India in 1975 for Canada—so the India he evokes is that of the 1960s and 1970s. More specifically it is Bombay of that era that he has recreated in this novel. Another significant aspect of this discourse is the leitmotif of "journeying"—which is also central to most Diasporic writing.

The three epigraphs which preface the novel set the tone. The first is from Firdausi's Iranian epic, *Shah Nama*, and recalls both the glorious Iranian heritage of a mighty Empire, as well as hints at the downgraded condition of present-day Parsis. The second one is from T.S. Eliot's "Journey of the Magi" and reminds readers of the ancient Zoroastrian religion and the belief that the magi who attended the birth of Christ were Zoroastrian priests. This epigraph also provides the title as well as the central metaphor of the novel—"A cold coming we had of it,/Just the worst time of the year/For a Journey, and such a long journey." Finally Tagore's lines from *Gitanjali* sum up the way in which the Parsis have moved from one country to another and how they have had to adapt themselves to new realities.

In *Such a Long Journey*, the Parsi world gradually moves out of its self-imposed isolation and interacts at the highest levels of finance and politics with the postcolonial Indian world. The catalyst which brings about this contact is the "factional" character of Major Jimmy Billimoria. This is a composite character fashioned out of the real-life State Bank cashier Sohrab Nagarwala and the Parsi agent from RAW (arm of the Indian Secret Service), who was close to Mrs. Indira Gandhi, the then Prime Minister of India. The story-line, however, is more centrally concerned with the events that had overtaken Nagarwala. He was the man involved in the Rs. 60 Lakhs scam that had rocked the Indira Gandhi Government in 1971. He claimed that he had received a call from the Prime Minister instructing him to hand over that large sum of money to a messenger. This was never accepted by the Prime Minister's Office and Nagarwala was charged with embezzlement and arrested. He died in rather mysterious circumstances before he could be brought to trial. The missing sum of money was also connected with the 1971 war between India and Pakistan, which resulted in the creation of Bangladesh.

It is against this backdrop that Gustad Noble and his family live out their lives in the city of Bombay. Mistry has here provided an "insider-outsider" view of Bombay. From the vantage point of the 1990s, Mistry has reviewed Bombay of the 1960s and 1970s. These were decades that witnessed the slow erosion of the idealism which had marked the beginning of the end of the Nehruvian dream of a secular India. The Chinese attack of 1962 was seen as a betrayal by Nehru. He never recovered from the shock of seeing his vision for Asian socialism and regional cooperation crumble.

The end of the Nehruvian Utopia also marked the beginning of sordid power-politicking, corruption at the highest levels, nepotism and cynical manoeuvring of the electorate. In Bombay, it marked the end of the island-city's famed religious tolerance. When large parts of Northern and Eastern India were convulsed by Hindu-Muslim riots in 1947, Bombay had remained an oasis of calm and sanity. This, however, changed in the 1960s with the rise of extreme right-wing political parties like the Shiv Sena. The Sena raised the bogey of "the other"—the religious other, the Muslim, the linguistic other, especially Tamil speakers, and the regional other, those who came from other parts of India.

Mistry, like many political analysts and novelists (see Rushdie's *Midnight's Children*), places the blame for this at Indira Gandhi's door— "How much bloodshed, how much rioting she caused. And today we have that bloody Shiv Sena, wanting to make the rest of us into second-class citizens. Don't forget, she started it all by supporting the racist buggers." (39)[15] The language of this denunciation of Mrs. Gandhi's politics is indigenized in the tradition of postcolonial discourse. Mistry's texts are splendid celebration of the Parsi idiom and faithfully capture its rhythms. Unlike earlier Indian English writers, notably Nissim Ezekiel, Mistry does not use Indian English to merely create a comic effect. He uses it consistently and naturally and thereby conveys its present status as one of the several Indian languages with its own distinctive phonetic and syntactic features—a part of the phenomenon of global "englishes." This is a postcolonial mode of resistance offered by other writers too—like Salman Rushdie, Michael Ondaatje, Upamanyu Chatterjee, Bapsi Sidhwa. They use the colonizer's language "not to curse with," but to subvert the privileging of colonial discourse and the hegemony of Master Narratives of the West, thereby most effectively sabotaging the unequal Prospero-Caliban dichotomy.

In the midst of this city, slowly succumbing to the triple-headed monster of religious, linguistic and regional chauvinism, stands the Khodadad Building, the Parsi residential complex where the main protagonists of the novel live. Significantly enough, the building is protected from the outside world by a high black wall. The wall is an important symbol in the text. It is actually a cluster of symbols—at the beginning of the narrative it represents both protection and reduction. It shuts out the outside world, thus providing security, but at the same time it reduces contact with the Indian reality. Outside the protecting/imprisoning wall lies the squalor of India—"the flies, the mosquitoes, the horrible stink, with bloody shameless people pissing, squatting alongside the wall. Late at night it became like a wholesale public latrine." (16)

As the novel progresses, Gustad Noble turns the offensively stinking wall into "the wall of all religions." He gets a pavement artist to paint on it gods and prophets of all the major Indian religions. "Over the next few days, the wall filled up with gods, prophets and saints. When Gustad checked the air each morning and evening, he found it free of malodour. Mosquitoes and flies were no longer quite the nuisance they used to be." (183) However, in the cynical, increasingly intolerant city, Gustad's wall is doomed. The Municipal Corporation pulls it down to widen the road and the gods come tumbling down. However, the artist takes this destruction quite philosophically. To Gustad's question about where he would go, he replies: "In a world where roadside latrines become temples and shrines, and temples and shrines become dust and ruin, does it matter where?" (338) The artist's mood is typical of the Hindu ethos which does not place much faith in external symbols of divinity and which is why in decolonized India there was no immediate vendetta-campaign to right the old wrongs, i.e. pull down mosques and churches, which had been built over temples. The destruction of the Babri Mosque in December 1992 was a politically-engineered event rather than an expression of the spontaneous religious belief and outrage that it was made out to be.

The destruction of Gustad's wall is turned into a positive happening because it prompts him to take down the blackout papers he had pasted on his windows and ventilators at the time of the Chinese attack in 1962. "He stood upon the chair and pulled at the paper covering the ventilators. As the first sheet tore away, a frightened moth flew out and circled the room." (339) This letting in of the light can be seen as a metaphor for the letting in of Indian reality into the cocooned isolation of the Parsi world. The tearing down of the blackout sheets could also signal a readiness on the part of the Parsis to let the Iranian past go and to let "new melodies break forth from the heart; and where the old tracks are lost, new country is revealed with its wonders."[16]

NOTES

1. In the tenth century CE, some Zoroastrians from Khorasan, a province of North Eastern Iran, left their homeland following the Arab conquest. They did so to avoid forcible conversion to Islam and religious persecution. They sailed to India and established themselves at Sanjan, Gujarat, on the North Western coast in 936 CE. These Zoroastrians came to be known as Parsis or Parsees in India, after Pars, the name of a province in Iran.

2. Amongst postcolonial Parsis writers are Bapsi Sidhwa, Boman Desai, Farrukh Dhondy and Dina Mehta.

3. V.S. Naipaul and David Dabydeen write from the West Indian diaspora, M.G. Vassanji writes from the African diaspora, Salman Rushdie and Farrukh Dhondy (among others) write from the UK diaspora. Bharati Mukherjee represents the USA diaspora and Vilas Sarang the Petro-dollar one.

4. See Salman Rushdie, *Imaginary Homelands* (London: Granta Books, 1991), pp. 10-11.

5. Present-day Parsis speak Gujarati which has developed from Nagar/Gujar between the 10th and 12th centuries CE. When the Parsis made their pact with the

ruler Sanjan, Jadav Rana, the local language was Apabhransh Bhasha or Old Gujarati.

6. Behram Malbari, *The Indian Muse in English Garb* (1876), *Gujarat and Gujaratis* (1882), The *Indian Eye on English Life* (1895) and Cornelia Sorabji's *Love and Life behind the Purdah* (1901), *Sun Babies* (1904), *Between the Twilights* (1908), *India Calling* (1935), *India Recalled* (1936).

7. Edward Said, *Culture and Imperialism* (London: Chatto and Windus, 1993).

8. Salman Rushdie, *Imaginary Homelands*.

9. Frantz Fanon, *Black Skins, White Masks*, with a foreword by Homi Bhabha (London: Pulo Press, 1986).

10. See interview by Ali Lakhani with Rohinton Mistry at the Vancouver International Writers' Festival, *The Long Journey of Rohinton Mistry.*

11. Rohinton Mistry, *Tales from Firozsha Baag* (1987; Rupa reprint, 1993); *Such a Long Journey* (1991; Rupa reprint, 1991).

12. See E. Kulke, *The Parsees in India: A Minority as Agent of Social Change* (Delhi: Vikas, 1978).

13. *Agiary* means a fire temple. However, Parsis are not fire-worshippers. For them fire is a symbol of purity and light and therefore representative of Ahura Mazda, the Supreme Lord.

14. A pejorative term used by Parsis for all Indians but it specifically refers to people who live in the Western Ghats.

15. When fascist parties like the Sena took over the streets of Bombay and enforced their writ through strong-arm tactics, minorities like the Parsis felt particularly threatened. In post-Ayodhya India though, the attention of the Hindu right-wing parties is focussed on Muslims and other not so visible minorities have got a brief respite. Also, given the minuscule number of Parsis (only 100,000 world wide and 70,000 in Bombay), they have never been a high-visibility minority in India. It is only in Bombay that their concentration and high level of education and expertise make them a threat to the job-prospects of what the Sena call "the Sons of the Soil."

16. See epigraph from Tagore's *Gitanjali* in *Such a Long Journey*.

This article was first published in *Journal of Commonwealth Literature*, Vol. XXX, No. 2, 1995.

Parsi Culture and Vision in Rohinton Mistry's *Such a Long Journey* and Firdaus Kanga's *Trying to Grow*: A Comparative Study

N.P. SHARMA

The present article proposes to look at the anguish and the angularities of the Parsi way of life in the limited context of Rohinton Mistry's *Such a Long Journey* and Firdaus Kanga's *Trying to Grow*, both of which are not only the brilliant first novels by two very promising Parsi writers, but they are also wrapped up in thick coverings of Parsi ethnicity behind and below which is visible the essence of the Parsi spirit.

The Paris: Past and Present

Parsis have been in India now for more than one thousand years. To say that they have not assimilated themselves with the mainstream is readily and easily belied by appearances of things. They have repaid the cost of the home India gave them many times over, by playing very important roles in every crucial development of life—Politics (Dadabhai Naoroji and Sir Phirozeshah Mehta), Industry (Jamshedji Tata), Science (Homi Bhabha), Law (Nani A. Palkhivala) and Music (Zubin Metha). Their contribution in creative writing and education is no less. This is not to say that the super immigration-friendliness India has in its blood had no role in these achievements. All the same, they are very patriotic, as is clear from the words of Dadabhai as quoted by Palkhivala in his book: "Whether I am a Hindu, a Mohmedan, a Parsi, a Christian or any other creed. I am above all an Indian. Our country is India, our nationality is Indian."[1]

Though marvellous, the Parsis are a moribund community, eighty to ninety per cent of which resides in Bombay, which is the locale of the two novels examined here. They are an endangered community crouching in their own sacrosanct and inviolable corners to exist as best as they can with a halo of break-but-not-bend sort of dignity and hauteur. It is feared, they are on their way out, as Aditi Kapoor warns in an article, "The Parsis; Fire on Ice" in *Times of India* (14 May 1989): "Unless something is done to augment their fast depleting numbers and to revive their religion, the Parsis after an illustrious past could well just fade out in oblivion."

This perception of the situation is shared by the renowned Parsi solicitor Palkhivala, who says it is entirely upto the present generation of Parsis to decide whether "they will become a decadent community with a glorious past, a perilous present, and a dim future." (320) The paper reciprocates the concerns and comments upto them in the light of the two novels under study.

Intertextuality in the Two Writers

On surface, the two writers are walking along their own different and unmeeting routes. Mistry sweeps over the whole India through Bombay and Kanga is concentrated on his personal predicament as he copes with and suffers it in Bombay.

There is in the two novels, what is technically called 'intertextuality' i.e. reflection and repetition of the experiences and ideas of one writer in the other. A minority-hence-powerless-group writer in whatsoever he writes is relatable to the race and a majority-hence-powerful-group writer tends to individualize, a point very neatly made by Nirmaljeet Oberoi: "intertextuality is a potent factor in a minority group because . . . the powerless group feels the need for support."[2] Their personal profile becomes one of the race. The conscious autobiography of the writer becomes the unconscious autobiography of the race. The individual and the race merge.

From this angle, these two widely different novels converge to similar ideas and points and thus make an interesting study.

The Parsi Vision in the Two Novels

(i) The Urge to Return to the Fountain

The two writers keep returning to the shreds and traces of the lived and hoary past, which even the extra-modern characters in the novels in vain fight against. They are helplessly tied to what they are trying to disentangle themselves from. They feel fallen in the Lake of Fire with an irretrievable Heaven lost behind. They emote over their attachment to their daglis, kustis, sadras, shops, schools, charity trusts, Tower of Silence and its vultures, the Davier where the richest Parsis live, their immaculately clean houses with red-tiled roofs and so on. This is their paradise. They would live and get lost in it rather than leave it. They are facing a grim 'to be or not to be' crisis of existence.

(ii) Religion: The Loosening Grip

Kanga presents girls talking about what the priest has under his white muslin robe in the 'choli-ke-piche' style in the fire- temple. And it is here that his parents have their romance. Kanga comments on these temporal affairs making inroads into the highest Parsi seat of spirituality: "We Parsees don't take our religion too seriously; those who do are considered downright dangerous and a little mad."[3] But the way Sam and Sera, the parents, behave in the novel only disproves the statement. Their valour in showing profound humanity to a son with permanently unworking legs, for which he dedicates the book to them, comes out of their religion. In *Such a Long Journey*, Gustad comes under the soothing and gentle sway of the death-time prayers and listens to them reverently, though he is not able to understand a word of them.[4]

Thus religion is no nonsense and Parsis should think twice before throwing the baby with the bath-water in the name of modernity and unorthodoxy.

(iii) The Tower of Silence

'The Tower' is, rightly or wrongly, the central symbol of the Parsi culture. The two novels reveal the doubleness of the Parsi vision about it.

If Mistry says, "Such a ghoulish system . . . ill became a community with progressive reputation and forward thinking attitude," (317) Kanga has one character say: "What do you suggest? . . . That we are burned to ashes, like those Hindus? Or chewed by worms like the English men? I, for one, prefer to be eaten by vultures." (73-74) The two writers let the 'Tower' come into their picture of life and hardly seem to reject it.

(iv) Drive towards Elitism

Ascension to higher intellectual echelons is a fond Parsi obsession and pursuit. In *Such a Long Journey*, Gustad's sense of lostness at his son's throwing over a chance of admission to IIT is pathetic, even tragic. It was like taking the crutch from the cripple. (55)

In the same way Brit's heroic struggle to get educated in *Trying to Grow* and his parents' loving involvement in it are novel efforts to fight crippling misfortunes in life.

But put into the backdrop of Parsi vision of life, they are symbolic of the Parsi propensity to elitism on the ashes of physicality. Ironically, is Brit not the symbol of the Parsi community that grows over-size brains on match-stick bodies, leading to depletion of their numbers—a mere one lakh now? It is time they reversed their priorities and produced more babies than books.

(v) The Reluctant Indians

The Parsis are too refined, too sophisticated, too highly cultured to merge seamlessly with the down-to-earth Indian masses. A character of *Trying to Grow* says in a culinary context that "we are reluctant Indians" (27) and it amounts to a Freudian slip. Another character in the same novel uses yet another revealing expression: "Anglophile, the Parsee disease." (161) This also is a factor that estranges them from India. All three Indians so far elected as MPs in England were Parsis. The fact insinuates to us their foreignness. Maybe, they feel a little rootless in India. And growing and rootlessness go ill together.

Their being a little uncomfortable in what is now their only HOME in the world does create a sense of insecurity among them. Look at the following self-evident quotations from *Such a Long Journey*:

(a) And today we have that bloody Shiv Sena wanting to make us second class citizens. (39)
(b) Parsi crow-eaters, we'll show you who is the boss. (39)
(c) Wait till the Marathas take over then we will have a real Gandoo raj. (73)

The charges galore: Indira nationalized banks because Parsis ruled the roost in banks (38); Feroze's heart attack was not really a heart attack (197), and so on. A.G. Khan in his book counterblasts the charges by asking: "What are your grievances, Mr. Mistry? Are they genuine or exuberance of 'Parsi' psyche?"[5]

(vi) Sex: Butchering and Bursting

Both Mistry and Kanga have been generous in sprinkling their

books with obscenities. But these burstings are due to the washed-in-
dettol, 'zero-b' goody-goody girls:

> Not like our Parsi girls with all their don't touch here and don't
> feel there fussiness. Everything they would open up. In every
> gully-gutchy, yaar, in the dark, or under the stairs, what what went
> on. (*Journey*, 91)

> . . . but it was such a relief when Jimmy died. We were only to-
> gether for two years and of that I was free for nine months and for
> the forty days after that, till my purification bath. (*Trying*, 35)

They marry too late (Mr. and Mrs. Manekshaw, *Trying*) to have any
fruitfulness. Not only this, it explodes into homo-sexuality and
indiscriminate sex (Amy, Ruby, Cyrus, Dolly, Defarge and Brit,
Trying). In *Journey* Tehmul commits a rape on the doll Roshan got as a
school-prize (301) and mother and daughter share the porno-mag, *The
Playgirl* in *Trying*. The characters move between too controlled and too
uncontrolled sex.

Parsis do need better sex-management. For them sex is more duty
than fun.

(vii) Suffering and Death

Suffering and death are the two most loved motifs in the two novels. In *Trying to Grow*, Brit suffers out of all proportion—born a pigmy
with 'Osteogenesis Imperfecta,' he broke his bone eleven times before
he was five, was toothless, was never able to walk and became the
'Heaven on Wheels,' crawled naked out of bath room till fourteen, had
to make do with music and books, had no regular school or friends of
picnics, on puberty became a sex-maniac, was deserted by friends and
left alone, losing sister by marriage and parents by death. Sufferings
make him grow. He watches 'I' as 'he' and realizes that loneliness is the
ultimate human destiny: "No, Amy, I've got to be alone. I have to be
Osteo Brit and not mind." (233)

In *Such a Long Journey*, we have the disreputable and cursed spinster Miss Kutpitia who lost her widower brother and his son for whom
she remained unmarried and who was her reason for living. Her tears
have all been cried long ago and grief needed no longer unburdening because it was accepted as part of life.

Dinshawji, the virgin prostitute and a pimp to the pleasures of life, is another character of *Such a Long Journey* to see life for what it is worth. The vultures that make short business of us in life are too many and too relentless. The corpses in the Tower of Silence are lucky because they face the ordeal only once. He laughs away the tears and tortures of life. He lives the joke of life laughing and dies so.

Thus these protagonists of life's tragedy face the ironies of life with the dispassion of a 'Yogi' and for them what is, is just 'is' and what is not is, just 'is not.' The visionlessness is their vision. What they value and what really sustains them is love and nothing but love.

The centuries of suffering, segregation and loneliness have brought the Parsis to a vision of life where nothing is amiss and perhaps this is how they are ready even for their extinction.

Such a Long Journey, shortlisted for the Booker Prize, *Tales from Firozsha Baag* and now his crashing *A Fine Balance* are no mean achievements by any standards for Mistry, the Indian now settled in Canada. The Bombayite Parsi journalist Firdaus Kanga's *Trying to Grow* followed by his impressive *Heaven on Wheels* are accomplishments of high promise. That is to say, both of them are writing at the highest of their powers and are compulsively readable. And yet (repeat yet) the Jungian Collective Unconscious is going to bob up everything they write. Canadian or Indian, they remain Parsis. No mosaic and no multiculturalism can cut man off the roots he sprouts and sucks sustenance from. So the writer of Indian origin Bissoondath's declaration in *Selling Illusions* that he wants to be defined as a Canadian[6] is yet another unsaleable illusion.

NOTES

1. Nani A. Palkhivala, *We, the Nation: The Lost Decades* (New Delhi: UBS, 1994), p. 320

2. Nirmaljeet Oberoi, "Intertextuality in the Poetry of Indians in Canada," *Indian Journal of Canadian Studies,* IV (1995), p. 68.

3. Firdaus Kanga, *Trying to Grow* (Delhi: Ravi Dayal, 1990), p. 14.

4. Rohinton Mistry, *Such a Long Journey* (Delhi: Rupa, 1991), p. 247.

5. A.G. Khan *Canadian Literature and Indian Literature: New Perspectives* (New Delhi: Creative, 1995), p. 17.

6. *Indian Journal of Canadian Studies,* IV, p. 17.

Modes of Resistance in the South-Asian Novel: A Study of the Fiction by Bapsi Sidhwa, Rohinton Mistry and Yasmine Gooneratne

GITA VISWANATH

I n the South Asian context, the category of class would necessarily collude with that of caste. Race manifests itself in the representation of the colonizer i.e. British and the neo-colonizer i.e. American, whose operative fields are both the economic and the cultural. Gender, the defining category of feminist discourse, cannot be treated in an isolated manner. Culture-specific contexts within which to locate the politics of gender provide broader parameters for investigation. Gender would thus subsume the categories of class and race in an inseparable way. Susie Tharu and K. Lalitha in their Introduction to *Women Writing in India* point out: "It was in the women's movement that a critique of culture first emerged as a viable political program. Consistently extended, this attention to the minute, everyday practices of subordination and expropriation has implications for the politics of class, caste, colonialism, ethnicity and a whole range of other structures of domination that determine the lives of women—and men." (30) These categories reveal the dynamics of power structures within hierarchies. I shall attempt to show in this paper how the authors I have selected for analysis—Bapsi Sidhwa, Yasmine Gooneratne, Rohinton Mistry—deploy the categories of class, race and gender not only to reveal their operations in hierarchical structures, but also as modes of resistance to established hegemonies. The idiom of resistance is central to all political reading of texts.

Bapsi Sidhwa's novel *The Crow Eaters*, set in pre-independence India, excels in its representation of a combination of Indian and British characters. Faredoon Junglewallah uses public space in his business and social interactions, while his spirited and indefatigable mother-in-law, Jerbanoo may be located in the private space of the home and body. Yet, it is Jerbanoo who is the more active agency of resistance to male/colonial power. As a much respected member of the Parsi community in Lahore, the power of speech is made available to Faredoon. So, his resistance is limited to its articulation through statements like, 'The sun will rise and set in their asses.' But for Jerbanoo whose protestations are ignored and trivialized by male instituted terminology like 'Nagging,' coupled with her forced confinement to a room in the house of the Allens in London, the benefits of speech are denied to her. So, the doubly marginalized Indian woman must create her own space for registering protest against the curbing of her freedom which by extension would also signify the lack of freedom for India. Being the oppressed subject, with no legitimate space for resistance, Jerbanoo makes her own body the site for generating protest. Her deliberate and meticulously planned act of defecating on the landing of the staircase in the Allen household in London is not mere scatalogical indulgence on the part of Sidhwa. This act becomes a trajectory of resistance from the dual categories of race and gender, which achieves at least momentarily a subversion of power structures.

In Sidhwa's other novel *The Pakistani Bride*, Zaitoon, a young girl is victimized by the debilitating patriarchal prescriptions of an insular tribal society. The woman is held as repository of moral values in a patriarchal society. Within this ideological framework, Zaitoon signifies the 'woman-as-victim' paradigm in much feminist writing. But the novel is not a mere study in victimology. Zaitoon frames her resistance in the gesture of defiance. Her escape from her husband and his family is the only act of Zaitoon propelled by her own free will, after being a victim of ineluctable fate almost throughout the narrative. Carol, the American girl in the story married to a Pakistani army officer is equally oppressed in her relationship. But the means of resistance being more easily available to her, due to her privileged class and race identity, she decides to break free. The open-ended novel makes available to the reader various options to construct its likely end. But there are strong pointers in the text towards Carol taking charge of Zaitoon and perhaps returning to America. The end of the novel achieves the feminist utopian ideal of female solidarity of sisterhood.

Ice-Candy Man is a reinscription of male texts on the Partition, which valorizes objective reality in the narrative and ignores the experiential realm of the woman. Sidhwa uses again the 'woman-as-victim' paradigm but here the victimization is a result of a collective action viz. the communal riots that followed the Partition. Riots are largely orchestrated by males. The riots become a signifier of a collective male victimizer. The maid in the Parsi family at Lahore whose address inscription in the novel is 'Ayah' is the one who suffers the impact of Partition the most. The story of the Partition is synecdoched in the story of the 'Ayah.' Her body is commodified by her own husband who admits her into a brothel. The riots give the Ice-Candy Man, later Ayah's husband, the opportunity to engineer her abduction. It is the narrator Lenny's Godmother who, with the help of the Recovered Women's Camp, liberates 'Ayah' by ensuring her safe return to Amritsar and reunion with her family. Hence, *Ice-Candy Man* and *The Pakistani Bride*, in extolling female solidarity cover much the same conceptual ground.

Female solidarity may be theorized in Rajeswari Sunder Rajan's words in her book *Real and Imagined Women*: "the typical female subject of feminism has been the subaltern woman or specifically the woman-as-victim, whose subjectivity post-structuralism has helped conceptualize discontinuous, heterogeneous, changing and contingent, or, as we may say, less than one. The fractured identity of this subject may enter into alliances with groups, which then makes possible a feminist politics. The collectivity represents her from the premise of a shared, universal experience of oppression and handicap i.e. powerlessness." (119) Significantly, even within this utopian sisterhood lies an in-built power structure, and this is where categories of class, race and gender collude with each other. Both Carol in *The Pakistani Bride* and the Godmother in *Ice-Candy Man* belong to the privileged upper class who assert precisely this upper class identity in rescuing the less privileged Zaitoon and Ayah. The narratives close at this juncture and do not explore the likely power politics that operate in the relationships that are formed within these hierarchies.

Such an exploration of the class/caste problematic is offered by Rohinton Mistry's *A Fine Balance*. The shift in the profession from cobbler to tailor negotiated by Om and Ishvar is the act of resistance to the curse of untouchability associated with the Chamar community. With a professional shift, a spatial movement also occurs. The tailors' movement from the village to the city which is an apparently classless space; and their entry into the life of Dina Dalal, a middle-class widow struggling to survive independently, make available to the reader to critique these events in the plot of the novel on grounds of representation of class. Most relationships delineated in the novel are symbiotic relationships. Class distinctions are shown as erasing themselves and members of different classes even transgress sanctioned spaces in need based equations. The notion of the family undergoes a redefinition in the novel, when Dina Dalal is forced to house the homeless tailors along with Maneck, a student who is her paying guest. Dina is quite clearly the head of this family, thus offering resistance to the norm of patriarchy. The tailors who initially are not allowed to eat in Dina's house or use her bathroom begin slowly to be given the permission to enter these forbidden spaces, thus co-opting them into her life not for any great humanitarian or egalitarian cause, but for the successful running of her own garment business. Dina's elder brother Nusswan who is the head of her maiden family after her father's death derives the authority of a father and couches his dominance in the rhetoric of protection. Dina's gesture of defiance is inscribed in her insistence on living alone and earning independently. For a while Dina's new 'family' and her economic empowerment create an idyllic space where no class distinctions exist. But the narrative (significantly that of a male), unable to sustain feminist individualism, coupled with classlessness is ruptured at this stage not by an individual, but the state in the form of the Emergency which is the historical backdrop to the novel. In the Indian socio-cultural field of signification, the nation is iconized as female (Bharat Mata). It is also not without significance that the Emergency was imposed by a woman Prime Minister. So, the nation as female with woman leader becomes the agent of oppression of the masses. Women (represented by Dina), the lower classes (represented by the tailors) and idealistic youth (represented by Maneck) are the worst victims of state sanctioned violence. The violence is targeted at the income-generating capacity (in Dina's case), at the body (as in the tailors' case one of whom is castrated through the sterilization program) and at the mind (as in the case of Maneck who is led to suicide). Such an unleashing of violence during the tenure of a woman leader may be explained by using Rajeswari Sunder Rajan's argument: "Successful women who 'make it' do so as a result of internalising male norms, and in turn are conferred honorary malehood largely in a gesture of tokenism." (105) The conferring of 'honorary malehood' removes the possibility of judging the Emergency on grounds of gender. The woman merges with the State and her actions may be seen as the exercise of power on the part of the state machinery, the identity of which is created by its supposedly male qualities of aggression and oppression.

Dina Dalal's ultimate return to her brother's household prioritizes the norm of the male-headed family. This defeatist end constructed by a male writer for Dina is of significance in feminist analysis. The single woman, imaged as helpless and incapable must therefore be restored to her 'rightful' place i.e. within the family structure. Dina is reduced from female individualist to feminine subject. This restoration to the family brings with it a re-emergence of class distinctions revealed by the back door entry of the tailors (now reduced to beggars on the streets of Bombay) for a quick afternoon meal before the return of Dina's brother. Here lies my quarrel with Mistry's *A Fine Balance*. In narrating the nation to borrow Homi Bhabha's alliteration, Mistry restores the balance towards the maintenance of the status quo which is in favour of patriarchy and a hierarchically stratified society. Mistry attempts neither intervention nor resistance in order to reinscribe the text with the politics of change. Instead, he merely offers his text at the altar of realism.

Speaking of the realist novel of the nineteenth century, Susie Tharu and K. Lalitha point out how it 'set up the world as home for its bourgeois hero.' "Its objects were delineated from his perspective in his image and the world was ordered in his interest. Realism was an effect of his gaze." (XI, 32) In the South Asian context in general and Mistry in particular, the 'gaze' is clearly that of urban, upper-class male.

Interestingly, Sri Lanka's foremost woman writer, Yasmine Gooneratne's novel *The Pleasures of Conquest* offers resistance not merely to patriarchy but patriarchy as it was historically constituted by class and colonialism. The novel engages in a rewriting of the national narrative by employing all the three categories of class, race and gender. Stella Mallinson, the American university teacher of creative writing, represents the neocolonizer's dream of cultural and economic conquest of the Asian sub-continent. Stella's mission in the island involves writing and the championing of the politically-correct environment cause. Her Asian experience is coloured by what Edward Said calls 'the textual attitude.' He goes on to say in his seminal work, *Orientalism*: "a white middle-class Westerner believes it his human prerogative not only to manage the non-white world but also to own it."

The Pleasures of Conquest is the locus of such a racial politics at work. The journal maintained by John D'Esterey, a nineteenth century British officer posted on the island called Amnesia, the biography of John D'Esterey by researcher Phil Destry and his Asian assistant Leila Tan, Stella's *Nine Jewel Rice*, an anthology of stories by nine writers— all these sub-texts within the novel penetrate into each other, each staking a claim to superiority. All their attempts are ultimately repudiated by Mallika's ballads and autobiography. Mallika is a maid in the house of Kumari who incidentally was one of the writers being shaped by Stella for her *Nine Jewel Rice*. Mallika's autobiography as narrated to her employer Kumari is preluded by the colophon in which she traces with great pride her geneology which reflects the essentially syncretic and pluralistic nature of the island nation. Mallika's autobiography is also the site within which notions of history are reconstituted. History becomes in the Lyotardian sense the Eternal present, in which colonial period is appropriated into its present and not abrogated as in normative texts of postcolonial literatures. Gooneratne's foregrounding of Mallika's text dethrones the Western hegemonic order from its position of power. All the other discourses in the novel narrativized by a 'superior' subject i.e. white, upper-class, male/female are ousted from the centre with Mallika's text successfully negotiating a shift from the periphery to the centre. This is achieved by one whose subjectivity may be defined as Asian, working-class woman. The hidden political agenda in women's writing surfaces quite clearly in Gooneratne's *The Pleasures of Conquest* as well as her earlier novel *A Change of Skies.*

A Change of Skies, generically an immigrant novel, addresses the immigrant experience from the contested margins of gender, race and nation. Here, resistance may be located within the everyday experiential realm of the private space of the protagonist, Navaranjini, who becomes Jean in Australia to facilitate easier assimilation. To put it in the words of Gayatri Spivak, "So intimate a thing as personal and human identity might be determined by the politics of imperialism." (*Three Women's Texts and a Critique of Imperialism*) Jean enacts a shift from the private to the public space through the publication of a cookery book, thus using artifacts from her private space to enable an escape to a space that redefines her subjectivity. The parallel narrative in the novel contained in the journal of Grandfather Edward, closes with return of the native to his homeland. In contrast, Jean's daughter Veena's visit to her native land is only holiday. Total assimilation with an alien culture is effected in the novel in a seemingly benign manner; but not before redefining the notion of assimilation as one which allows space for difference, so trenchantly revealed in the name of Jean's daughter. Christened Edwina after Edward, her great-grandfather, she chooses to be called Veena in daily communication; reversing her mother's name-change from Navaranjini to Jean. Spivak's anguish may be converted to hope that so intimate a thing as personal and human identity might be determined by indigenous culture.

It is modes of resistance such as those investigated above that charge subaltern writings with the power to question and contest existing paradigms, reinscribe normative texts and create new fictions, thus vocalizing zones of silence and illuminating areas of darkness.

From behind a Fine Veil:
A Feminist Reading of Three Parsi Novels

NILUFER E. BHARUCHA

Parsi women have not been rigorously subjected to the regimen of the Purdah, but they share the limited and reductive world of their Hindu and Muslim sisters in India. Parsi traditions are rooted in the patriarchal society of ancient Iran and these patriarchal moorings have been reinforced by a 1300 year long residence in India.[1] Association with the British during the Raj coated some Parsis with a thin patina of westernization and emancipation,[2] but for the majority of Parsi women the fine veil remained, from behind which they looked at the world. As Sherry B. Ortner has put it: "the secondary status of woman in society is one of the true universals, a pan-cultural fact."[3]

Child marriages, truncated schooling and multiple childbirths were till recently the lot of most Parsi women. Bapaiji, in Boman Desai's *The Memory of Elephants*,[4] belongs to this group of repressed women. She is hemmed in by an oppressive world which she determinedly pushes aside to create her own female space, but is not quite successful.

Lenny, the girl-child narrator of Bapsi Sidhwa's *Ice-Candy Man*,[5] inhabits a more sophisticated cityscape, as compared to the rural universe of Bapaiji. However, she too is subject to the limitations of her gender. In fact she is a doubly marginalized figure—female and physically handicapped. Lenny, from behind this veil of marginality, offers a uniquely subaltern view of the bloody birthing of Pakistan. This view is as strong an indictment of patriarchy as it is of colonialism.

Soul-destroying, mindless drudgery is the destiny of Dilnavaz in Rohinton Mistry's first novel, *Such a Long Journey*[6] Dilnavaz hovers at the periphery of the novel as her domestic crisis assumes national importance. Her husband—the man—is an active participant in this crisis but she is the hapless spectator. She can only take recourse to superstition and prayers, as her beloved eldest son drifts away from the family and her husband's life is endangered by minister elements outside her control.

This paper examines the world view provided by these Parsi women from behind the veil of patriarchy, marginality and haplessness and at- tempts a feminist reading of the three novels under study.

Two of these novels, *The Memory of Elephants* and *Such a Long Journey* are written by men, while the author of *Ice-Candy Man* is a woman. The paper also explores the difference this has made to the presentation of women characters in these books.

Desai's *The Memory of Elephants* begins with a section entitled 'Bapaiji.' Bapaiji is the Gujarati word for grandmother. The portrait of Bapaiji reveals the many female stereotypes, most writers harbour about their women characters. This is in spite of the fact that Desai's Bapaiji is apparently a 'strong' woman and Desai's male protagonist Homi, grudgingly admires her for this. This strength and admirable qualities, however, are related to Bapaiji's 'man-like' nature and behaviour—she is almost an honorary man. This tendency of attributing male, and hence superior, characteristics to a female character, happens when in the "creation of fictions, writers call upon the same signifying codes that pervade social intersections, representing in fiction the rituals and sym- bols that make up that social practice."[7]

What is, therefore, required is a reading of the novel which will go beneath the surface of the man-like Bapaiji and seek what Adrienne Rich has called "the true knowledge of women" which comes from "uncovering the hidden, making ourselves present . . . [and defining] a reality which resonates to *us*, which affirms *our* being."[8]

In *The Memory of Elephants*, the male protagonist, Homi, lives in a disoriented world upon which the Memo-Scan he has invented, imposes its own order. This Memo-Scan give him the 'memory of elephants, the memory of whales, the equation of the universe.' It is an instrument which activates the collective unconscious of the Parsis, what Bapaiji calls the 'memory of the soul.' Bapaiji is Homi's guide through the in- tricate maze of racial memory. She is not just Homi's past, she is also the Parsis' link with rural India. She is a symbol of those first Parsis who had made a pact with Jadhav Rana, the king of Sanjan, who had given them refuge in Gujarat. The pact had included among other things, a promise to embrace the local language,[9] customs and clothes. So Bapaiji speaks only in Gujarati to Homi, whom she calls her 'Ameri- can grandson.'

When the novel opens, Bapaiji is already dead, but 'speaks' to Homi from 'the Kingdom of God.' However, Bapaiji's voice is that of a man. In the magical realism of Desai's novel, Bapaiji is, in the 'hereaf-

ter,' a man. Bapaiji has shed what the male world considers a 'restrictive' female body: 'I am a man here; I wear pants, I walk more quickly,
upright, directly forward without that ridiculous waddle with which so
many women are afflicted, without those huge breasts like a cow ele-
phant's which always got in my way; I even have a deeper voice—you
will doubtless find this comical, but it is what I had always wanted, to
be a man, to do things men did.' This is a classic example of what Kate
Millett has termed the "expected traits of minority status: group self-hatred and self-rejection."[10] In a man-dominated world, women, irrespective of their class/caste, are minority figures, who believe in the male-
version of the inferior attributes of women and as a result hate themselves.

Bapaiji's definitive statement also opens up various avenues of investigation, the most important of which are the questions of gender-
identity and male taboos/disgust connected with the female body.

A flashback to Bapaiji's childhood in Navsari, a small town in
Southern Gujarat, reveals an early dissatisfaction with her feminine
identity. As Millett says, the fact of being female is a biological reality,
the matter of feminine identity is a matter of sociological conditioning.
Bapaiji, from early girlhood, waged a battle against the constriction of a
feminine identity. She is what Heilbrun has called a "male-identified"
girl.[11]

Bapaiji plays tag and 'Hu-tu-tu' with the boys and is unembarrassed
when her skirt rides to her thighs. She defies social expectations and refuses to identify with her mother. She takes to wearing her brother's
pants in an effort to rid herself of the restrictions of her sex. By putting
on male clothes, she also indirectly seeks to put on the power that goes
with being a man.[12]

With approaching adolescence, Bapaji finds it increasingly difficult
to ignore her female body and begins to consider it an encumbrance to
her fantasy of being a boy. She soon finds herself married off to the
staid Hormusji Seervai. Hormusji had been married earlier to a girl who
had a baby by someone else. The marriage had been annulled and 'the
baby made to drink milk.' Here we are in a social milieu where child
marriages and infanticide were a reality.

This marriage 'made a woman out of Bapaiji' and she hated it. The
reductive existence of the youngest daughter-in-law in a patriarchal
family jars on Bapaiji. She is subjected to all the taboos patriarchy imposes on female sexuality—isolation during menstruation, segregation
from unrelated males, etc. Bapaiji nearly revolts against these sanctions
but cannot subvert her husband's deep-rooted faith in the partiarchal

system. And since Bapaji cannot imagine a revolt outside the matrix of male approval, she is unwillingly subdued.

However, the most restrictive bondage is imposed on her by motherhood: 'She had hated pregnancy and she hated motherhood; it was just one more way, perhaps the most diabolical, of tying down a woman.' Chodorow says that societies "ensure an adequate supply of child-tenders by encouraging all women to be empathic and nurturant."[13] Bapaiji resists being the nurturant female.

With the arrival of middle-age, Bapaiji involves herself with the local affairs of Navsari, attends meetings and makes speeches. Yet she turns down the invitation to be on the governing board of an institution, 'Fifteen years of domesticity had tamed Bapaji to the point of questioning a woman's role outside the home.'

In her later years Bapaiji is given the title of Rajya Ratna by the Maharaja of Baroda, for the services rendered to Navsari. In spite of these successes, achieved as a woman, Bapaiji wishes herself into becoming a man after her death. The restrictions she had faced as a girl and woman, the fights she had to wage against a suffocating patriarchy, make her turn against herself—against her identity as a woman. It is only by becoming a man that she can finally shed the restrictive veil which had impeded her existence as a woman.

Bapsi Sidhwa's girl-child Lenny in *Ice-Candy Man* is rather different from Bapaiji. She is the creation of a woman writer. Gubar has remarked: "If artistic creativity is likened to biological creativity, the terror of inspiration for women is experienced quite literally as the terror of being entered, deflowered, possessed, taken, had, broken, ravished— all words which illustrate the pain of the passive self whose boundaries are being violated."[14] The woman writer is like Charlotte Bronte, who suffers a 'secret, inward wound.'

These are rather perceptive remarks in the context of Sidhwa's novel and her protagonist. Here Lenny experiences through the surrogate character of her Ayah, the terror and trauma of rape, as her world is shattered and the boundaries of her universe violated.

Sidhwa's novel, like Desai's, is technically sophisticated. It was post-modernist characteristics of fantasy and the fragmentation of time. It also employs the device of allegory. As Mihai Spariousu says: 'Allegory appears whenever there is an overload felt so overwhelming that it can only be dealt with in a multiplicity of dimensions.' As allegory, the novel operates at a different level from that of a pure narrative.

Ice-Candy Man is set in the partition period when the colonizing power, presented her erstwhile Empire with the parting gift of a yet-toheal wound, i.e. the partition of India into the two nations of India and Pakistan. Lenny, the girl-child is herself a wounded creature. She is maimed by polio. Thus to the biological disadvantage of being female in a male world, are added the handicaps of a physical deformity and a colonial milieu. The novel could thus be interpreted as a political allegory.

However, it also operates as a feminist allegory. Through the character of Lenny, Sidhwa explores a female universe hemmed in by the restricting and reductive forces of patriarchy and colonialism.

The novel begins on this note of restriction and reduction, 'My world is compressed. . . . My child's mind is blocked by the gloom emanating from the wire-mesh screening the oblong ventilation slits [of the Salvation Army wall]. I feel such sadness for the dumb creature I imagine lurking behind the wall. I know it is dumb because I have listened to its silence, my ear to the wall.' This capacity to 'listen to silence,' to create text from a negation, is the special gift of women writers who are denied articulation in a man's world. It is also significant that this silence is experienced in relation to the Salvation Army wall—the Salvation Army bringing the civilizing message of a colonizing power to the dumb Calibans of this earth.

Sidhwa's opening pages also stress other woman-related issues. Lenny, unlike Bapaiji is not male-identified. She has strong female models with whom she has a woman-to-woman bonding. This is in keeping with current psychological theories of a girl-child's positive bond with her mother. Lenny identifies with her Godmother: 'The bond that ties her strength to my weakness, my fierce demands to her nurturing, my trust to her capacity to contain that trust—my loneliness to her compassion—is stronger, than the bond of motherhood. More satisfying than the ties between men and women.'

Lenny also shares a strong bond with her mother and her Ayah. Both these women also possess the strong female qualities of Godmother—strength, a capacity to trust and be trusted, nurturant natures and compassion. These two women also share with all other women the pressures and pains inflicted by a male world.

The mother blames herself for Lenny's polio: 'I'm to blame.' she says, 'I left her to the ayahs.' Here she is a victim of social expectations *vis-a-vis* the female as a nurturer. The Ayah become a victim to the politics of rape and is violated and humiliated like countless other women in that apocalyptical year of 1947, caught in the crossfire between rampant patriarchy and callous colonialism.

Lenny's world is also populated by other deprived female characters. Papoo is the daughter of Muccho, the sweeper woman, who considers her to be a nuisance and a curse. The maltreatment of Papoo by Muccho runs through the novel like a malevolent strand. Muccho is a victim of a patriarchal society which has engendered a fierce self-hatred in her, which manifests itself in violence against her daughter whom she sees as an extension of herself. She finally marries Papoo off to a middle-aged dwarf. This is the ultimate wound she inflicts not just on her daughter, but also on herself.

The question of education and the female-child, is also touched upon in this novel. Lenny's handicaps are piled one on top of the other and her lameness is allied to her femaleness, to deprive her of a proper education. The doctor tells her parents, 'she'll marry—have children—lead a carefree, happy life. No need to strain her with studies and exams, he advises: thereby sealing my fate.'

Thus deprived of schooling, Lenny is thrust more and more into the company of her Ayah with whom she explores the multi-faceted world of Lahore. It is this association which forms the core of *Ice-Candy Man*.

Through the agency of the Ayah, Lenny is awakened to a frank appreciation of female sexuality. The Ayah is assiduously courted by a cross-section of men in Lahore. The favoured suitor is the Masseur whose clever fingers 'massage Ayah under her sari' till 'she moans, a fragile, piteous sound of pleasure.' From these moments of vicariously shared excitements, Lenny discovers the 'secret rhythm of creation and mortality.' It is through the Ayah and her many admirers that Lenny also learns of betrayal, pain and violation.

The idyll which Lenny and Ayah share with the Masseur, the Afghan knife-sharpener and the Ice-Candy Man is abruptly shattered as India is torn apart into two bleeding nations. The fantasy of romantic love is shattered and Ayah, the chivalrously-courted beloved, becomes the victim of a male conflict. Overnight the secular landscape of Lahore is fragmented into religious enclaves. 'One day everybody is themselves—and the next day they are Hindu, Muslim, Sikh, Christian. People shrink, dwindling into symbols. Ayah is no longer just my all-encompassing-Ayah—she is also a token—a Hindu.' As a token[15] Ayah is raped by her erstwhile Muslim admirers and friends. She is abused in retaliation for the trainloads of dead Muslims and bags full of the breasts of Muslim women cut off by Hindu men. As Millett has put it, rape is an offence 'one male commits upon another—a matter of abusing "his woman." The Ayah become a victim of these sexual politics allied to the carnage set off by a departing colonial power.

The most tragic aspect of the abuse of Ayah is that it is set off by Lenny's 'truth-infected tongue.' It is Lenny who betrays Ayah to the mob which had come looking for her at Lenny's house. Taken in by the blandishments of the Ice-Candy Man, 'Don't be scared Lenny Baby. . . . I'll protect Ayah with my life!' Lenny gives away her hiding place and sees the Ice-Candy Man change before her eyes and knows that 'I have betrayed Ayah.' Here Lenny is like Muccho who betrays her own daughter into male bondage. A betrayal, the result of centuries of patri-archal conditioning, a misplaced faith in the integrity of men and a sear-ing lack of confidence in and hatred for the female self.

The much-loved Ayah now becomes what Lenny's boy-cousin calls 'the opposite of Virgin Mary'—a whore. As a whore she is outside the pale of 'respectable' society. Lenny is kept away from her as her mother and Godmother strive to 'rehabilitate' Ayah and thousands of other vio-lated women like her. Women, who like Hamida, Lenny's new Ayah, have become untouchables because their husbands 'do not like other men to touch their women.'

Ayah is by the end of the novel married to the Ice-Candy Man, who professes to be desperately in love with her. But having been betrayed by him, Ayah prefers to go back to her family in Amritsar—which is now in India. In a final, sinister sentence, Sidhwa tells us that the 'Ice-Candy Man too disappears across the Wagah border into India,' thereby underlining the ever-present nature of the betrayer.

Rohintom Mistry's *Such a Long Journey* tells the tale of Gustad No-ble who is unwittingly caught up in the world of Indian politics and mired in the quicksands of high finance and war-mongering that accom-panied the Indo-Pak conflict of 1971. The book is based on the real-life scandal involving Sohrab Nagarwala, the State Bank cashier, who was at the center of the 60 lakh rupees scam which had rocked the Indira Gandhi government.

In this novel the domestic life of Gustad Noble clashes with the forces of money—capitalism. Trapped in this crossfire is Dilnavaz, Gus-tad's wife and their children. This is very obviously a novel written from the male point of view. It opens with Gustad Noble saying his early morning prayers and closes with Noble's belated action of tearing off the black-out papers from his ventilators and windows—thereby symbolically letting in light and reality. It is the male characters in the novel who 'act,' who 'do' things—Gustad, his sons, major Billimoria— a thinly-disguised Nagarwala, the sinister underworld figures of Ghulam Mohammed, the Christian friend Malcolm and the Bank cashier Din-shawji. Even the retarded and lame Tehmul initiates some action.

The female characters are the passive recipients of the results of these actions. Dilnavaz, her daughter Roshan and their neighbour Miss

Kutpitia are female stereotypes much beloved of male writers around the world. Like the secondary status of women, female stereotypes are also a pan-cultural phenomenon. Dilnavaz is the perfect foil to Gustad— soft and pretty, where he is big and muscular. As a couple they exhibit the typical features of male aggressiveness and female passivity. As Millett has sarcastically noted: "If aggressiveness is the trait of the master class, docility must be the corresponding trait of a subject group."

The child Roshan is a doll-like creature, sickly and fragile. She is in direct contrast to the sons Sohrab and Darius. She has neither the mental prowess of Sohrab nor the physical robustness of Darius. As is the wont of female children, she cries, gets scared and is petted and cosseted by Daddy.

Miss Kutpitia (her name in Gujarati means the 'quarrel-some one') is the archetypal spinster, much reviled by the neighbourhood. She is 'the ubiquitous witch of fairy stories come to life,' Mistry informs us. Miss Kutpitia could have been a strong character, privy to ancient wisdom of women, living a life of independence. However, all we get is a caricature of a silly, superstitious woman. Miss Kutpitia's spells and magic, her being a 'witch,' is not at all in a positive feminist sense.

Instead her magic spells are reduced to being a mere manifestation of women's irrational nature. Mistry pokes fun at this 'inferior' female behaviour. Miss Kutpitia, being a spinster and a little batty is to be allowed her superstitions. However, Dilnavaz, the happily-married woman, a 'fulfilled' mother's belief in Miss Kutpitia's 'jadu-mantar,' is indirectly attributed to her concern and love for her husband and children. So, whenever she is not cooking, filling water or settling quarrels between her husband and their son Sohrab, she is found conspiring with Miss Kutpitia in creating spells for the well-being of her family. Sohrab's intractability is sought to be removed by a spell involving a lizard's tail. Limes, chillies, alum and even poor Tehmul are pressed into service to cure Roshan's illness.

Gustad, the rational male, is never party to this 'mumbojumbo.' His mind is occupied with more important matters of national importance— how to legalize the large sums of money sent by Major Billimoria. He is not house-bound like Dilnavaz. He ranges as far as Delhi.

Dilnavaz's universe is on the other hand the restricted world of her home and she ranges only as far as Miss Kutpitia's flat. Her role is that of wife, mother and home-maker; she cooks, serves and withdraws discreetly while the men discuss politics. Unlike Lenny she is not even aware of them. Nor does Mistry attempt to probe beneath the surface of the reductive lives of Dilnavaz and Miss Kutpitia. He does not attempt to seek the reasons for their belief in spells, instead there is an exploitation of their 'stupidity' for comic effect. The pathos underlying Miss Kutpitia's lonely life, or Dilnavaz's drudgery is not explored. Indeed the pathos and sympathy in the book is reserved for the eponymously named Gustad as he nobly strives for the welfare of his family. There is even empathy for the retarded Tehmul as he copulates with Roshan's stolen doll but not a silver of sympathy is thrown the way of Miss Kutpitia. Maybe her stridency and apparently unbalanced behaviour too were caused by repressed sexuality. Mistry, however, is not willing to concede sexuality to his female characters. Dilnavaz interacts only in a Romantic way with her husband, not sensually, or even worse, sexually! Miss Kutpitia is celibate in the cause of an orphaned nephew, who eventually dies and little Roshan, unlike Lenny, is neither troubled nor curious about her body.

In the novel entitled *Such a Long Journey*, the female characters in it do not journey at all. They remain stationary while the world around them moves and changes. Theirs is a static universe where they are even denied the knowledge of their own stultification and repression by their creator. This novel which is a fictional account of recent history is in the genre of what Greene and Kahn have called history as 'written by men, from a male perspective. What has been designated historically significant has been deemed to according to a valuation of power and activity in the public world.'

Such writing disregards the 'histories' of the Dilnavazs, Miss Kutpitias and Roshans. These women have to emerge from behind the veil, to speak, to fill in the blank pages of their stories. It is feminist, woman-centered readings which will help in tearing this veil to shreds so that a Bapaiji may exist proudly as a woman, instead of aspiring to be a man and a Lenny's universe is not subjected to the brutality of repeated violence.

NOTES

1. The present-day Parsis are descendants of the Zoroastrians who fled Iran around 800 A.D., after its invasion by the Arabs. They fled to avoid forcible conversion to Islam and took refuge in Gujarat, on the Western coast of India. Here they were given refuge by the King of Sanjan, Jadav Rana, on the condition that they neither proselytize nor wage wars. These Zoroastrians were called Parsis in India, after their language, Farsi. The name Parsi could also be traced to the Persian province of Pars, from where these people were presumed to have come.

2. In British India, unhampered by the taboos of the Hindu caste system and the isolationism of the Muslims, the Parsis surged ahead and became the most westernized was mainly confined to men. Even though some rich Parsis educated their daughters, who became doctors, lawyers and teachers, the majority of Parsi women received little education and were subjected to the taboos and repressions of a strict patriarchy.
3. Sherry B. Ortner, "Is Female to Male as Nature is to Culture?," in Rosaldo and Lamphere, ed., *Woman, Culture and Society* (Stanford: Stanford University Press, 1974).
4. Boman Desai, *The Memory of Elephants* (London: Andre Deutsch, 1988).
5. Bapsi Sidhwa, *Ice-Candy Man* (U.K.: Penguin Books, 1988).
6. Rohinton Mistry, *Such a Long Journey* (London: Faber and Faber, 1991).
7. G. Greene and C. Kahn, *Making a Difference: Feminist Literary Criticism* (New York: Methuen, 1985).
8. Adrienne Rich, "Taking Women Students Seriously," in *On Lies, Secrets and Silence: Selected Prose 1966-1978* (New York: Norton, 1979).
9. The language spoken in Gujarat is called Gujarati. It belongs to the Indo-Aryan group of languages. However, this modern day Gujarati developed only around the 15th century AD. At the time the Parsis made a pact with Jadhav Rana, the local language was Apabhransh Bhasha or what Grierson (quoted in Rawal Anantrai, *Gujarati Sahitya*, 3rd ed., Bombay: Macmillan, 1968) called Old Gujarati. It was from Old Gujarati that Nagar/Gujar was derived between 10th and 12th century AD; modern Gujarati developed from this Nagar/Gujar language.
10. Kate Millett, *Sexual Politics* (New York: Doubleday, 1969).
11. Carolyn Heilbrun, *Reinventing Womanhood* (New York, 1979).
12. Sandra Gilbert, "Costumes of the Mind: Transvestitism as Metaphor in Modern Literature," in E. Abel, ed., *Writing and Sexual Difference* (Sussex: Harvester, 1982).
13. Nancy Chodorow, *The Reproduction of Mothering* (Berkeley, 1978).
14. Susan Gubar, "The Blank Page and the Issue of Female Creativity," in E. Abel.
15. The Ayah's character can also be interpreted as a symbol of the Indian earth and that of the titular Ice-Candy Man as the ravisher—the conquerer(s) of India. (For details see N.E Bharucha, "The Parsi Voice in Recent Indian English Fiction: An Assertion of Ethnic Identity," in V. Sarang and N. Bharucha, ed., *Indian English Fiction 1980-1990: An Assessment,* Delhi: B.R.)

Local Colour in *Tales from Firozsha Baag*

S. RAMASWAMY

T o establish the context for the tell-tale discussion of 'local colour' in Rohinton Mistry's *Tales from Firozsha Baag* (Rupa, 1993), perhaps the best opening would be a few lines from one of his own 'tales'—"Swimming Lessons":

> Mother and Father read the first five stories, and she was very sad after reading some of them, he said he must be so unhappy there, all his stories are about Bombay, he remembers every little thing about his childhood, he is thinking about it all the time even though he is ten thousand miles away, my poor son, I think he misses his home and us and everything he left behind, because if he likes it over there why would he not write stories about that, there must be so many new ideas that his new life could give him. (243)

Jane Austen is supposed to have advised an aspiring writer: "If you haven't gone to Ireland, don't send your hero there." Rohinton Mistry is an insider to Firozsha Baag, Bombay and his vignettes are naturally totally authentic. Ironically perhaps he is able to achieve this authenticity as he has distanced himself by emigrating to Canada so that he can produce the effect of an insider/outsider to a scene every detail of which is etched and engraved in his mind. Remembering, re-enacting, re-creating that place-time-people with accuracy, understanding, and insight is the vision of Rohinton Mistry. This note is only a cursory look at three of his short stories in his *Tales from Firozsha Baag*. In a manner of speaking, this is a "comedy" of manners and Firozsha Baag is Mistry's "Malgudi." At least as far as this collection is concerned, he is an R.K. Narayan in making. The five stories briefly looked at here are—"Auspicious Occasion," "One Sunday," "The Ghost of Firozsha Baag," "Of White Hairs and Cricket" and "Swimming Lessons."

Firozsha Baag is a new locale in the literary horizon which takes shape stroke by stroke in each story. With the skill of a miniature painter, Mistry peels off layer after layer off the residents of the Baag just as from the walls of Baag in A Block: "something would have to be done about peeling paint and plaster; in some places the erosion was so bad, red brick lay exposed." (7) The residents of the Baag lie totally exposed in an excellent "exposition." Mistry has an eye for detail and the vignettes are executed with a deft hand where the local colour is totally authentic. This is in evidence in all the 'Tales'; but for the present comment, only five tales are taken into consideration.

II

"Auspicious Occasion" is 'Behram roje.' The Parsee community of Bombay is the focus of attention and the husband and wife Rustomji and Mehroo are analyzed with keen insight. The husband, twenty years older than the wife, after many years of marriage and in spite of his "toothless gummy mouth" glances salaciously at the young charwoman Gajra surreptitiously peeking from behind the newspaper—*The Times of India*—which serves a useful purpose—hoping for his wife to be away so that he can be a little more bold or a little less inhibited in his ogling adventures at home. He is quite prepared to believe a similar attitude to women in others, for example, in the priest Dhunjisha, whom he suspects to be an "old goat." Though his pious wife doesn't want him to say "nasty things about such a holy figure," (12) Rustomji is convinced that Dhunjisha was quite capable of slipping in lewd remarks between lines of prayer." (14) Mehroo goes to the prayer meeting on the "auspicious occasion" of the title of the story, discovers that the old man has been murdered and returns home. Meanwhile, Rustomji who stirs out in his gleaming white sees red! "His starchy whiteness aroused in him feelings of resplendence and invincibility." (14) This is alas, short-lived as he receives his full quota of betel nut juice aimed at him from the upper deck passenger in the Bombay bus. This is a different kind of 'murder'—the colour red is imaginatively transplanted from the murder in the "cathedral" to a symbolic 'murder.' This is also a hand of fate—actually the "mouth of fate"!—"On the upper deck sat fate in the form of a mouth chewing tobacco and betel nut, a mouth with a surfeit of juice and aching jaws crying for relief. And when the bus halted at Marine Lines, fate leaned out of the window to release a generous quantity of sticky, viscous, dark red stuff. . . . The squirt of tobacco juice caught him between the shoulder blades: blood red on sparkling white." (16-17)

The blood-red pan on the dugli of Rustomji and the red blood on the body of the murdered priest are connected in an interesting juxtaposition. The quarrel that ensues between the enraged Rustomji and the irate mob provides a quasi-funny situation where very native choice abuses are hurled about contributing to local colour and an increase in the Indian-English vocabulary. The generous sprinkling of 'native' words throughout the tale makes it not just Indian but also specifically 'Parsi' whose life at the Firozsha Baag is being authentically re-created by Mistry—Behram roje, dugli, pheytoe, navjote, dhandar-paato, sali-boti, loban, ailchee, chasni, Ashem Vahoo, etc.

"One Sunday" introduces us to a few characters connected with Firozsha Baag and to the neighbouring Tar Gully life. Apart from the boys of the Baag, Kersi and Percy, we are introduced to the outsider, odd-job man—thief, Francis. Najamai's Sunday outing from the Baag to visit her sister's family at Bandra proves quite eventful. The neighbours of the Baag, Tehmina and the Boyces add to the furthering of the 'local colour.' The eroticism that runs through the narratives of Mistry appears here too:

> When Najamai's daughters had gone abroad, they took with them the youthful sensuality that once filled the flat and which could drive Kersi giddy with excitement on a day like this, with no one home, and all before him the prospect of exploring Vera and Doll's bedroom examining their undies, that invariably lay scattered around. . . . Now, exploration would yield nothing but Najamai's huge underclothes. (29)

Tehmina's memories are of a different sort: "From downstairs came the strains of 'The Blue Daumbe.' Tehmina swayed absently. Strauss! The music reminded her of a time when the world was a simpler, better place to live in, when trips to Tar Gully did not involve the risk of spit globs." (32) The evocation of the atmosphere of the Tar Gully is the counterpoint to the life of Firozsha Baag, with its 'mutka' and 'ghatis.' The pursuit of the thief Francis down the Tar Gully provides the racy conclusion to this tale.

As far as the narrative technique is concerned, two tales, "Of White Hairs and Cricket" and "The Ghost of Firozsha Baag" are specially interesting. "Of White Hairs and Cricket" is a sort of autobiographical reminiscences from boyhood—a form of recollection, not entirely in tranquillity. The narrator is a fourteen-year-old boy. He remembers his father, mother and grandmother—'mamaiji.' A Sunday in Firozsha Baag is reconstructed—presented in bits and pieces while the boy is "uprooting the signposts of mortality," while his 'nimble' fingers are wielding the tweezers, pulling out the white hairs from his daddy's scalp. The Sunday in Firozsha Baag is looked at in terms of the other residents too—reinforcing the 'local colour.'

However, "The Ghost of Firozsha Baag" is my favourite. It is a triumph of narration. The narrative technique is extremely interesting as it is in the individualistic language and style of an "ayah" from Goa—a devout Catholic. The life of Firozsha Baag is observed here from an outsider's point of view—from the point of a simple, honest, uneducated 'outsider.' The English that is used by this person is both authentic and quaint. The narrator's personality comes through loud and clear with all her background, upbringing, humility, likes and dislikes, prejudices and essential unsophisticated honesty and innocence. The narration reminds one of the use of the West-Indian dialect in Samuel Selvon's stories, especially *Brackley and the Bed.* The creative use of an authentic dialect, different from the 'standard' English is an interesting aspect of commonwealth writing, taking us back to the discussion of the subject by Kenneth Ramchand in his chapter "The Language of the Master?" in his *The West Indian Novel and its Background.* The utter simplicity of the narrator is reflected in the story as well as the way it is narrated.

> After reaching first floor I stooped to rest. My breath was coming fast-fast. Fast-fast, like it does nowadays when I grind curry *masala* on the stone. Jaakaylee, my *bai* calls out, Jaakaylee, is *masala* ready? Thinks, sixty-three-year- old ayah can make *masala* as quick as she used to when she was fifteen. Yes, fifteen. The day after my fourteenth birthday I came by bus from Goa to Bombay. . . . Now it has been forty-nine years in this house as ayah, believe or don't believe. Forty-nine years in Firozsha Baag's B Block and they still don't say my name right. Is it so difficult to say Jacqueline? But they always say, Jaakaylee. Or worse, Jaakayl. (44)

Jaakaylee's "ghost story" is special among ghost stories. This is a most connubial ghost—a 'bhoot' with a difference. The sly eroticism that has already been mentioned is evident even in this "ghost story." This dear simple ayah "always believed in ghosts": "When I was little I saw them in my father's small field in Goa." (43) But her Bombay ghost was different: "Once a week the ghost came, and always on Friday. On Friday I eat fish, so I started thinking, may be he likes smell of fish. Then I just ate vegetarian and yet he came. For almost a whole year the

ghost slept with me every Friday night, and Christmas was not far
away." (49) Mistry's mixture of eroticism and humour gives his whole
narration a light touch and a tongue-in-cheek bantering tone. Jaakaylee
goes on to confess: "I told Father D'Silva everything and then I was
feeling much better. Father D'Silva said I was blameless because it was
not my wish to have the bhoot sleeping with me." (50) And "Believe or
don't believe, the *bhoot* did not come. "Thus ends the Bhoot affair. The
Firozsha Baag bhoot was 'ashamed' because "Father D'Silva knew
about what he had been doing to me in the darkness every Friday
night." (50) But earlier to this end of the affair, the children in Firozsha
Baag would shout: "See today, at cinema R.K. Anand's fillum *Bhoooot
Bungla* starring Jaakaylee of Block B." (47) But Jaakaylee did not care.
"I knew what I had seen." (47) The climax—anti-climax—comes when
Jaakaylee herself is mistaken for a ghost by her employer, Bai. On a
cold night around 2 a.m. when Jaakaylee felt cold she covered herself
completely in her white bedsheet, her ears and head covered and went
out on the balcony when Bai and her husband came home and Bai
looked up and saw "the ghost"—with the result that after that "many
people" in Firozsha Baag started to believe in the ghost— including
Dustoorji of A Block, who came one day and 'taught bai a prayer.'

The racy narration, all in the language of the simple Goan Ayah,
makes this a remarkable achievement. The half-serious, half-mocking,
ironic tone, and the utter simplicity of the narrator's narrative technique
constitute a triumph in creating the local colour of Firozsha Baag's Parsi
community. In his "Swimming Lessons," Mistry allows himself a gen-
eralization on the Parsi community:

> Mummy used to take good care of Grandpa, too, till things became
> complicated and he was moved to the Parsi General Hospital.
> Parkinsonism and orteoporosis laid him low. The doctor explained
> that Grandpa's hip did not break because he fell, but he fell be-
> cause the hip, gradually growing brittle, snapped on that fatal day.
> That's what orteoporosis does, hollows out the bones and turns ef-
> fect into cause. It has an unusually high incidence in the Parsi
> community, he said, but did not say why just one of those mysteri-
> ous things. We are the chosen people where orteoporosis is con-
> cerned. And divorce. The Parsi community had the highest divorce
> rate in India, which is the result of the other? Confusion again of
> cause and effect. (230)

This last story in the collection, "Swimming Lessons" is exceptional in

the sense that we get a glimpse of Firozsha Baag from the
"outside"—from the distance of Canada in fact. The fact that the story
itself is printed in two types in print—ordinary and italics—is an
integral part of the narrative technique as in Faulkner's *The Sound and
the Fuzy*. The juxtaposition of India-Bombay-Firozsha Baag on the one
hand and the Canadian experience on the other makes this story a tale
apart. Imagery and symbolism are brought into the narration. The
first-person narration is in itself interesting:

> Water imagery in my life is recurring. Chaupatty Beach, now the
> high-school swimming pool. The universal symbol of life and re-
> generation did nothing but frustrate me. Perhaps the swimming
> pool will overturn that failure.
>
> When images and symbols abound in this manner, sprawling or
> rolling across the page without guile and artifice, one is prone to
> say, how obvious, how skill-less; symbols, after all, should be still
> and gentle as dew drops, tiny, yet shining with a world of mean-
> ing. But what happens when, on the page of life itself, all-
> engirdling sprawl of the filthy sea? Dew drops and oceans both
> have their rightful places; Nariman Hansotia certainly knew that
> when he told his stories to the boys of Firozsha Baag. (234)

Firozsha Baag and Canada are brought together in a "unified
sensibility" in the story "Swimming Lessons": "I examine the
swimming-trunks I bought last week. Surf King says the label, Made in
Canada-Fabrique Au Canada. I've been learning bits and pieces of
French by bi-lingual labels at the supermarket too." (235)

III

Obviously Rohinton Mistry is learning more than "bits and pieces"
in Canada and not just "French." No wonder this promising young
writer gave up a plush bank job to devote himself full time to writing. In
Tales from Firozsha Baag the "outsider" element is also effectively
used to further the "local colour" of Firozsha Baag.

The "Outsiders,"—Gajra the "Gunga" in "Auspicious Occasion,"
Francis the thief in "One Sunday," Jaakaylee the ayah in "The Ghost of
Firozsha Baag," the swimmers in "Swimming Lessons" all help in de-
fining the local colour of Firozsha Baag. The neighbouring Tar Gully,
Mehroo's outing on Behram roje, Rustomji's own misadventure, Na-
jmai's visit to Bandra and the goings on in her flat in her absence, the

pranks, the boisterous boys in the Baag, define the local colour in
graphic unmistakable detail:

> Plaster had been drifting for some years now in this A Block flat
> as it had been in most of the flats in Firozsha Baag. . . . When
> neighbours, under the leadership of Nariman Hansotia, had de-
> cided to *pool* some money and hire a contractor to paint the exte-
> rior of A Block, Rustomji, on principle, refused to hand over his
> share. The building had acquired an appalling patina of yellow and
> grey grimness. (6)

The inside of the building was no better. The description of the stairs,
the state of plumbing etc. plunges us into the interior landscape of the
Baag. The local colour—which the lack it literally—emerges in flying
colours! The metropolitan macrocosm of Bomaby and the Baag which is
the microcosm within it are so accurately and minutely pictured in the
manner of a miniature painter by Rohinton Mistry that this was what
won this teller of tales the literary prizes in Canada. The motto from
Thoreau that Mistry uses at the beginning of his book is very significant
and it illustrates his own method: "Not that the story need be long, but
it will take a long while to make it short."

This essay is not about expatriate sensibility and Rohinton Mistry's
immigrant Canadian "identity." So the reason for the "local colour" in
these *Tales,* whether it is nostalgia or just a writer's point of view and
technique, does not concern us here. However, the continuation from the
opening quotation from "Swimming Lessons" can be quoted in conclusion: "But father did not agree with this, he said it did not mean that he
was unhappy, all writers worked in the same way, they used their
memories and experiences and made stories out of them, changing some
things, adding some, imagining some, all writers were very good at remembering details of their lives." (243) This 'internal' personal statement best sums up Rohinton Mistry's achievement in *Tales.*

Geophysical Imagination and History in the Fiction of Rohinton Mistry and Bharati Mukherjee

NEELAM TIKKHA

L iterature reflects the social conditions and the historical evolution of the society. In a perilous enterprise, one does not discuss causes or motives. One is either a fighter or a deserter. In the centre of Canadian life is a dominating herd-mind in which nothing original grows. The human mind has nothing but human and moral values to cling to if it is to preserve its integrity or even its sanity, yet the vast unconsciousness of nature in front of it seems an answerable denial of those values that Joshua Marsden calls the "shutting out of the whole moral creation in the loneliness of the forests."

An immigrant to Canada, even though westernised, has a painful experience. He—is vexed with identity crisis—his natural hold of the indigenous culture unconsciously interferes with the logical grasp of alien culture. Indians, Africans and Caribbeans have strong indigenous cultures, but the great good place is 'somewhere else.' Sarosh dreams "Canada to be a land of milk and honey."[1] In this effort the immigrants land up in a place which is neither a paradise nor hell. They feel suspended in a limbo. The dedication to the set traditions and sense of belonging to their motherland comes in opposition with new environment resulting in desolateness and feeling of insecurity. The immigrant faces two questions "who am I?" and "where is here?" The latter question is due to the geographical and historical past of the country. Atwood's remark explicates the above proposition:

'Who am I?' is a question appropriate in countries where the environment, the 'here' is already well-defined, so well defined in fact that it may threaten to overwhelm the individual. In societies where everyone and everything has its place a person may have to struggle to separate himself from his social background, in order to keep from being just a function of the structure. 'Where is here?' is a different kind of question. It is what a man asks when he finds himself in unknown territory, and it implies several other questions. Where is this place in relation to other places? How do I find way around it?[2]

Canada seems a strange land even to Canadians. As Corall Ann Howells says, "Canadian writing has always been pervaded by an awareness of the wilderness, those vast areas of dark forests, endless prairies or trackless wastes of snow which are geographical facts and written into the history of Canada's exploration and settlement." The impact of the environment is so great that it sets out as major determiner of Canadian identity; John Moss calls it the "geophysical imagination." Landscapes described in poems, novels or short stories are seldom just about nature; they are "usually about the poet's attitude towards the external natural universe. That is, landscapes . . . are often interior landscapes: they are maps of a state of mind." Atwood comments that the North is always at the back of the minds of the Canadians and "Turning to face north . . . we enter our unconscious. Always in retrospect, the journey north has the quality of dream." (49) The wilderness both attracts and frightens. Gabrielle Roy calls it 'pure terrible country.' A look into the Canadian past establishes the fact that Canadians themselves suffer a "colonial cringe" and are terrified within their own country. Also, Indian immigrants to new lands face similar crisis not by chance but due to their legacy from the days of the British Raj. The immigrant experience is neither Indian nor Canadian, rather it is universal. Their country, their native culture comes into conflict with the foreign culture. Their traditional norms are censored and rejudged in the light of their puzzling alien environment. According to Matthew Arnold, they are "Wandering between two worlds, the one dead, other powerless to be born."

"Squatter" by Rohinton Mistry and "The Management of Grief" by Bharati Mukherjee are stories that portray such experience. These stories deal with the basic human emotion but reveal how the change in place and environment causes displacement and feeling of insecurity. Rohinton Mistry is a South-Asian Canadian writer. In the short story "Squatter," Sarosh an Indian from the Parsi community, living in a chawl called Firozsha Baag, decides to migrate to Canada and leaves India. His friends and relatives have a mixed opinion. Some appreciate his decision while others disapprove it. A heated debate ensues: some feel "What a smart decision he had made, that his whole life will change for the better; others said he was making a mistake, emigration was all wrong, but if he wanted to be unhappy that was his business, they wished him well." (154) In a jocular frivolity, he makes promise: "My dear family, my dear friends, if I do not become completely Canadian in exactly ten years from the time I land there, then I will come back. I promise." (155) His mother takes him to the prayer book and makes him swear that he will keep his promise. She advises him: "It is better to live in want among your family and your friends, who love you and care for you, than to be unhappy surrounded by vacuum cleaner and dish-washers and big shiny motor cars." (155) The friends also counsel him not to be embarrassed if he decided to return to the country of his birth. The swearing quells the debate and celebration goes on merrily. The ten-year-time-limit words said in light-heartedness, "hung over him with the awesome presence and sharpness of a guillotine." (155) Ten years later, Sarosh calls himself 'Sid' and is completely westernised in all respects except one—he is unable to use WC: "At first this inability was no more than mildly incommodious. As time went by, however, the frustrated attempts caused him great anxiety. And when the failure stretched unbroken over ten years, it began to torment and haunt all his waking hours. . . . He remained dependent on the old way and this unal-terable fact, strenghtened afresh every morning of his life in the new country, suffocated him." (154)

In the privacy of his home, Sid squats barefoot on the WC to get the cathartic effect. Elsewhere he carefully covers the seat with the toilet paper, the art he had learnt after the first time, when his shoes had left the tell-tale footprints on the seat. He had to clean it with a wet paper towel, fortunately no one noticed him doing that. But since the world of washroom "though" private is at the same time public. The absence of feet below the stall room, the smell of faeces, the rustle of paper, glimpses caught through the narrow crack between stall door and jamb—all these added up to one thing: a foreign presence in the stall, not doing things the conventional way. And if the one outside can re-ceive the fetor of Sarosh's business wafting through the door, poor un-happy Sarosh too could detect something malodrous in the air, the pres-ence of xenophobia and hostility. But Sarosh does not give up. He keeps trying to adjust: "Each morning he seated himself to push and grunt and push, squirming and writhing unavailingly on the white plastic oval. Ex-hausted, he then hopped up, expert at balancing now, and completed the movement effortlessly." (156) He later visits Indian Immigrant Aid So-ciety Dr. No-Ilaaz. He suggests him to implant small device called Crapps Non Interruptus, or CNI in the bowel, which would be control-led by an external hand-held transmitter similar to ones used for automatic garage door openers. This doctor is true to his name. He was able to dissuade his patients from following the very remedies which he first so painstakingly described.

The external maladjustment of Sarosh is the map of inner turmoil. It is not merely the western toilet but the xenophobia that makes his adjustment even more difficult in the foreign country. Xenophobia is confronted with the basic indigenous native culture of one's country resulting in alienation, desolation and loneliness. The light-hearted jovial story has serious undercurrents.

"The Management of Grief"[4] by Bharati Mukherjee establishes the fact that change in landscape necessarily implies change in sensibility. This creates a rift between the past and the present; if one tries to bridge the rift, it ends in sterile contemplation of the past since changes in the landscape rule out any possibility of 'connection.' In this attempt, the individual is alienated from oneself. In other words immigrants keep "surrendering little bits of a reluctant self every year, clutching to the souvenirs of an ever-retreating past." (2) In the story, Shaila Bhave, the woman-protagonist loses her husband and two sons in an airplane crash caused by terrorist bombing in 1985. Many Indo-Canadians lost their families in this. Outwardly well composed, she mourns the death of her sons and her husband. Her emotional control surprises those around her. Her sentiments are congruous with the cold country Canada itself. The response of Canadian police and diplomats is also cold and callous. They coldly inform the grieving people: "The plane broke into two. . . . Unconsciousness was instantaneous." (184) The Irish, on the other hand, provide free trip to the grieving people and flowers to the strangers.

When Shaila returns to India, she flutters between the two worlds. She is too old to give up one world and too young to accept the other world in totality. In search of peace, she travels to Varanasi, Haridwar, Kalighat, Rishikesh. She also seeks the help of palmists who offer her cosmic consolations, but ends up in buying a trip back to Canada. She is not aware where the voyage will take her, and where it will end. Like Sarosh, she will echo one day in congruity with the landscape: "The world can be a bewildering place, and dreams and ambitions are often paths to the most pernicious traps . . . life in the land of milk and honey was just a pain in the posterior." (168)

To conclude, the protagonists in the stories of Rohinton Mistry and Bharati Mukherjee are not unusual in experiencing schizophrenia under an alien sky; it is a commonplace and universal phenomena. The change in landscape implies change in culture and sensibility due to 'geophysical imagination.' The external problems like Sarosh's inability to use western toilets and Shaila's inability to let her emotions loose are merely the maps of mind and xenophobia.

NOTES

1. Rohinton Mistry, *Tales from Ferozsha Baag,* (New Delhi: Rupa, 1991), p. 168.
2. Margaret Atwood, *Survival: A Thematic Guide to Canadian Literature* (Toronto: House of Anansi, 1972), p. 17.
3. Coral Ann Howells, *Canadian Women Novelists of the 1970s and 1980s* (London: Methuen, 1987), p. 11.
4. Bharati Mukherjee, *Darkness* (Ontario: Penguin Canada, 1985).

Bad Faith in "Lend Me Your Light"

SUBHASH CHANDRA

Sartre's concept of Bad Faith occupies an important place in the existentialist paradigm of authenticity of self in hostile, despairing and life-negating environment. Doomed to exercise freedom of choice, as Sartre sees it, the self has to choose between one course of action and another (even not choosing and remaining passive signifies a choice) and then face the consequences of the choice. But how authentic one is in choosing or not choosing a course of action is a moot point, for one may invent attenuating circumstances/factors for justifying one's action/inaction. This act of manufacturing justificatory reasons is termed as Bad Faith by Sartre. In the present paper, I intend to examine the operation of Bad Faith in Mistry's story "Lend Me Your Light."[1]

The story begins with Tagore's words from *Gitanjali*: "Your lights are all lit—then where do you go with your lamp? My house is all dark and lonesome—lend me your light." These words of Tagore acquire a piquant poignancy in the context of the story which, when analysed, reveals the need for Indians to remain rooted to their soil, help their fellow brethren who are oppressed, deprived and exploited, but are completely helpless and at the mercy of the powerful. Most of the expatriate writers suffer from a sense of guilt, which gets reflected in their stories, because though all writing, to a certain extent, is a process of self-analysis and a search for answers, the expatriate writing is more so. The question: "Is it desirable to leave one's country?" therefore becomes a tangled puzzle, the unravelling of which involves anguish, nostalgia, guilt for the writers and their characters.

The reason for leaving one's country is always clear enough: better prospects and opportunities in the land of the plenty. But what is not foreseen by the migrant is the blurring of the definition of his own identity that is the unavoidable outcome of the transplanting process. Also what is not realised is the inauthenticity that comes to mark the lives of the migrants. Salman Rushdie, while talking of Guntur Grass, pinpoints the turbulence and turmoil a migrant goes through when he says: "A full migrant suffers, traditionally, a triple disruption: he loses his place, he enters into an alien language, and he finds himself surrounded by beings whose social behaviour and codes are unlike and sometimes even offensive to his own. And this is what makes a migrant such a pathetic figure, because roots, languages and social norms have been three of the most important parts of the definition of what it is to be a human being."[2] Rushdie goes on to say, "The migrant, denied all three, is obliged to find new ways of describing himself, new ways of being human." And in this process of acquiring a new self-definition, often confusion persists and Bad Faith is practised.

Reverting to Tagore's words, the less fortunate seem to be importunating their comparatively better off brethren not to leave them, because they need their help, their sympathy, their attention. The villagers, living in far-flung places are poor and exploited. They need the help of their educated fellow human beings to be taken out of the clutches of the oppressors. The writer highlights the moral failure of those who go away by the technique of comparison and contrast and seems to empathize with Percy who chooses to stay on in India and work among and for the villagers, even at the risk to his own life. But before taking up this contrast in detail, let us consider the case of comparison.

Of the three friends, Jamshed, Percy and Kersi (the latter two are brothers), Jamshed and Kersi leave for America and Canada (Toronto) respectively. The motives for migration are obviously material prosperity, better prospects for jobs and career advancement. The prospect of migration is a celebratory occasion and, therefore, Kersi receives plenty of congratulatory greetings and blessings on the occasion of his departure. The narrator-protagonist records: "Then the neighbours began to arrive. Over the course of the last seven days they came to confer their blessings and good wishes upon me." (178) Najama's blessings condense the general feeling: "Lots and lots of years you must live, see lots of life, study lots, earn lots, make us all very proud of you." (180)

Jamshed's letter from America to Kersi, who is in Canada dubs India a "dismal place" where "Nothing ever improves, just too much corruption" which is "all part of the *ghati* mentality" (*ghati* is an umbrella word for a person who is menial, low and all that is undesirable). Kersi wonders why Jamshed is so much full of "disdain and discontentment even when he was no longer living under those conditions." (181)

Interestingly, Kersi is irritated by Jamshed's condemnation of India. He tries to prove him wrong becoming a member of the Parsi-club and visiting Parsi get-togethers. He wants to be a part of India by participating in all that is Indian in Canada. His letter to Jamshed does not share Jamshed's contempt for India. But has Kersi found all the answers to the questions that trouble him as an immigrant? Is he at peace with himself as Percy is in India, trying to light the dark homes of the poor in villages?

Kersi's visit to India does not solve his riddles. Having defended India against Jamshed's criticism, he too indulges in Bad Faith. His words in this context reveal the truth: "Bombay seemed dirtier than ever. I remembered what Jamshed had written in his letter, and how it had annoyed me, but now I couldn't help thinking he was right. Hostility and tension seemed to be perpetually present in buses, shops, trains." (187) Mistry wants to make it clear that both these characters are being inauthentic, because he juxtaposes the pair with Percy—an individual whose self possesses integrity and authenticity. He, too, is living in the same Indian environment which is found to be insufferable by Jamshed and Kersi. If anything he is living in worse conditions, involving threat to his very life, because he is working in a village as a part of a group of young, enthusiastic persons, who help the credit-burdened poor farmers. But he does not make the hostile and uncomfortable conditions an excuse for leaving Bombay for abroad. On the contrary, he has, in the words of Tagore, decided to lend his light to the deprived whose houses are dark. So, the inhospitable conditions cannot be used as alibis, according to the norms set out in the text by the author. If one turns away from these conditions, it is because one does not choose to engage with reality. One does not have the courage to confront the contrary. To be authentic extracts some price. Percy is prepared to pay it. Jamshed and Kersi are not. But then people like Jamshed and Kersi pay another kind of price for being inauthentic. Confusion and misery afflict them. Kersi's self-definition remains fuzzy. He waits for an epiphany. But there are no epiphanies at the quotidian level of existence. One has to search for the answers. Jamshed also pays a kind of price. Why is he so pathologically angry with Bombay? Here is an example of his sizzling anger. He has accidentally met Kersi near the Flora Fountain during his visit to Bombay (Kersi also happens to have come). Pointing to the pavement stalls he fumes: "Terrible, isn't it, the way these buggers think they own the streets—don't even leave you enough room to walk. The police should drive them off, break up their bloody stalls, really." (190) He is angry with Bombay. In fact, he is angry with himself, because he suffers from guilt.

However, Percy is at peace with himself. The group of which he is a part, arranges interest-free loans for the farmers in the form of seeds and fertilizers at cheaper prices, from the cooperative they have formed. The exploitative system, entrenched in the village, feels threatened and commits violence. They kill Navjeet, one of members of the group. Percy is shocked, shaken and afraid. But the shock and the fear pass.

When the whole gruesome incident is related to Jamshed by Percy's mother, Jamshed's response is along the expected lines: "I told you from the beginning all this was a waste of time and nothing would come of it, remember? Every time we met we would talk about it, and you used to make fun of me wanting to go abroad. But I still think the best thing for you is to move to the States. There is so much you could achieve there. There, if you are good at something you are appreciated, and you get ahead. Not like here, where everything is controlled by uncle-auntie, and . . . " (192)

However, Percy discards Jamshed's selfish wisdom. He is no longer afraid. He turns to his mother and says in a quiet voice: "Could we have dinner right away? I have to meet my friends at eight o'clock. To decide our next move in the village." (192) Mistry obviously puts Percy on a higher pedestal in the story in relation to the other two. His authenticity is valorized. Jamshed with his guilt and anger and Kersi with his dichotomies, ambiguities and resultant confusions and blurred self, waiting for an epiphany are marginal human beings, practising Bad Faith.

NOTES

1.   Rohinton Mistry, *Tales from Firozsha Baag* (New Delhi: Rupa, 1993).
2.   Salman Rushdie, *Imaginary Homelands* (New Delhi: Penguin, 1991).

Such a Long Journey: A Critical Study

JAYDIPSINH DODIYA

R ohinton Mistry was born in Bombay in 1952. He emigrated to Toronto in 1975 where he worked for ten years in a bank, studying English and Philosophy part-time at the University of Toronto. He has won several awards for his creative work. His stories have been published in a number of Canadian literary journals and anthologies. These are published in book form in *Tales from Firozsha Baag*. He is also the author of two novels—*Such a Long Journey* and *A Fine Balance*.

The heart of the novel *Such a Long Journey* is Mistry's recreation of the life and times of Gustad Noble, an aging Parsi. Gustad, his wife Dilnavaz, their two sons Sohrab and Darius and daughter Roshan live in the Parsi residential colony of Khodadad Building in Bombay. Gustad is the grandson of a prosperous furniture dealer, a lover of books and tasteful living, whose fortunes were squandered by an alcoholic son, Gustad's uncle. Gustad's father was too gentle and weighed down by the sense of family loyalty to salvage his share of the inheritance. Gustad now works in a bank and lives in straitened circumstances, among other Parsis. His grandfather's taste survives in Gustad's nostalgic daydream of building a bookcase, in collaboration with his son Sohrab, to house his decimated collection of books. His father's goodness and compassion inform all of Gustad's actions and relationships which constitute the novel.

The inhabitants of Khodadad Building are representatives of a cross-section of middle-class Parsis expressing all the angularities of dwindling community. All the characters in *Such a Long Journey* are individualised and memorably drawn with humour and compassion.

The characters outside Khodadad Building who come alive in the pages of this novel are Gustad Noble's bank associate Dinshawji with his salacious puns and comic mask, his childhood friend Malcolm Saldhana initiating Gustad into the intricacies of western music and the miracles of the church of Mount Mary; the physician Dr. Paymaster forever unable to shed the name plate of his predecessor Dr. Lord; Peerbhoy Paanwala dispensing varieties of Paan and anecdotes to the visitors on their way to the cages of prostitutes, the unnamed pavement artist graduating to a wall-artist and back again; the bank manager Mr. Madan who is stingy in granting leave; the office peon Bhimsen collecting newspapers with photographs of Nixon and Kissinger for the toilet-training of the children in his Jhopadpatti.

The title *Such a Long Journey* comes from T.S. Eliot's poem "Journey of the Magi," which provides one of the three epigraphs to the novel:

> A cold coming we had of it,
> Just the worst time of the year
> For a journey, and such a long journey. . . .

There are few Indian English novels that have effectively used the backdrop of the post-independent Indian political context particularly of the crucial period of the sixties and the seventies. Rohinton Minstry portrays the picture of this period in this novel. The novelist offers commentary on the socio-political situation and raises a national debate on corruption in high places. Some characters in the novel make really illuminating comments. For instance Gustad thinks about the position of the Parsis in Bombay and comments thus: "No future for minorities, with all these fascist Shiv Sena politics and Marathi language nonsense. It was going to be like the black people in America—twice as good as the whiteman to get half as much." (55)

Regarding the change of the street names in Bombay, Dinshawji comments on the notion of displacement:

> Names are so important. I grew up on Lamington Road. But it has disappeared, in its place is Dadasaheb Bhadkhamar Marg. My school was on Carnac Road. Now suddenly it's on Lokmanya Tilak marg. I live at Sleater Road. Soon that will also disappear. My whole life I have come to work at Flora Fountain. And one fine day the name changes. So what happens to the life I have lived? Was I living the wrong life, with all the wrong names? Will I get a second chance to live it all again, with these new names? Tell me what happens to my life. Rubbed out, just like that? Tell me. (74)

Major Bilimoria's reappearance on the scene of action disturbs the already precarious position of Gustad. Through the enactment of

Nagarwala case, he makes an important political statement. Nagarwala received nearly sixty lakh rupees from a bank manager in Delhi, allegedly on the strength of a phone call from the Prime Minister which, it was said, he imitated. Nagarwala was dead after a few months. Nobody knew where the money went. Since this involved a member of Parsi community, the Parsis were considerably perturbed and the death of Nagarwala itself raised many eyebrows. Here is a view of a Parsi about the incident.

> The Nagarwala incident, because it involved a Parsi, jolted the self-image of the community no less. Having long ago lost their literature to the vanadalism of Alexander the Accursed, and their dance, music, art, poetry and even their language to the process of adapting to a new home in India the Parsis have developed a particularized culture culled from a mixture of ancient myth and legend overlaid by a life sustaining sense of recent achievement. Gratified to have earned an honourable place in the country of their adoption through their contribution to every field of endeavour and proud of having retained a strong ethical tradition the Parsis were deeply anguished by the ambivalent role Nagarwala had played in the sordid story.

On the whole, *Such a Long Journey* is Rohinton Mistry's masterpiece. It expresses the author's feelings about his community. This particular novel contributes in advancing the notion of Community Literature.

Bibliography

1. R.K. Dhawan, ed., *Indian Literature Today* (New Delhi: Prestige, 1994), Vol. I.
2. Nilufer E. Bharucha and Vilas Sarang, ed., *Indian English Fiction 1980-90: An Assessment* (New Delhi: B.R., 1994)
3. Rohinton Mistry, *Such a Long Journey* (New Delhi: Rupa, 1991).
4. Muriel Wasi, "Putting Magic into Realism," *The Hindu* (Literary Review), 4 July 1993, p. 1.

Such a Long Journey and Its Critical Acclaim

M. MANI MEITEI

Such a Long Journey (1991) is a novel which heralds Rohinton Mistry's arrival as a gifted writer. The book unfolds a long vista of varied interests all along the development of a well-wrought plot. Set against the background of the Indo-Pak war of 1971, it delves into the human predicament meted out to the central character, ruining all his hopes by circumstances beyond his control. Gustad Noble, the central character in the novel, is an individual depicted as a classical tragic hero, who is passing from "happiness to misery" and is pitted against heavy odds, which he faces almost with placid serenity. Side by side many things do not escape the novelist's serious concern. He cherishes the values of friendship, condemns the scourge of war, and denounces unscrupulous, corrupt and hypocritical political leaders who have eaten in the vitals of the nation. In a post-modernist tone, however, he refrains from becoming a political propagandist so that his work does not become a political mouthpiece. His frankness in exposing social and political ills of India is due to the fact that he has no political axe to grind. Furthermore, Mistry's strong opposition to social and class distinctions and his anguish over the environmental pollution have widened the spectrum of the contemporary gamut of reality the novel conveys.

Closely observed, *Such a Long Journey* is a novel deriving its form from the classical literary tradition. The novelist's predilection for the great tradition rather than for the modernist method of fictional experimentation with its emphasis on time and consciousness manifests his ideological stance of being a critical and socialist realist. In short, ideology mentioned here, denotes the literary mode adopted by the writer, that again operates at the level of its form and style. Mistry's *Such a Long Journey* is in line with the realist tradition in which the narrative is pushed forward in arithmetical progression and is chronological rather than spatial in the development of the plot. It gives comedy, tragedy, humour and satire. Along with them there lies a rich fabric of beliefs, superstitions, magic, rites, nationalistic ideas, humanism, radicalism, secular views and so on. In other words, it is life in its fullness, freshness and variety that the novel ceaselessly contemplates. Based on the sequential development of the plot the book offers a powerful narrative that keeps a sustained intensity throughout with a few surprising turns in order to effect a climax and also to precipitate the hero's fortune into a fall.

The grandeur the book attains is the creation of the central character, Gustad Noble, in whose life and suffering a large rhythm of universal pattern is carved out. Gustad's suffering is no suffering abstraction, for deep down it there is immense significance through which the novelist's high imaginative power to evince his vision that no happiness will last forever is implanted. Everything in the novel happens as if some immanent will is firmly set to counter human action as in an epic or a heroic tragedy. In spite of everything it is destiny that Gustad finds at the helm of affairs. Like Oedipus, he bows to the will of Providence, and not unlike Job, he finds in compassion and endurance a dignity and greatness withstanding all that fortune keeps in store for him.

In the opening of the novel Gustad is seen as a godfearing man, the envy of all: "Tall and broad-shouldered, Gustad was the envy and admiration of friends and relatives whenever health or sickness was being discussed" and although he had met with "a serious accident just a few years ago" even that left him with "nothing graver than a slight limp."[1] Comparatively, a happy man in his early fifties, Gustad is a bank employee and a father of three children, two sons—Sohrab, nineteen, Darius, fifteen—and a daughter, Roshan, nine years old. As the novel progresses, one finds Gustad's hopes, dreams and aspirations being blighted in a manner quite contrary to his likings. Without any moral depravity he incurs the frowns of fortune rendering him distraught and helpless: first, the sudden disappearance of Major Bilimoria from Khodadad building, who "had been like a loving brother" to Gustad and almost a "second father to the children" (14); second, his son Sohrab's refusal to enroll himself as an IIT student, whose bad manners and violent temper spoilt the ninth birthday party of Roshan, culminating in his desertion of his home; third, the protracted illness of Roshan, a complicated case of diarrhoea; fourth, Gustad's receipt of a package from Major Bilimoria and the trouble thereafter to hide ten lakh rupees; fifth, Gustad's close friend Dinshawji's illness and his eventual death; seventh, the death of Tehmul Lungraa, an idiot and retarded child, another inmate of Khodadad building; and the last, the destruction of Gustad's sacred wall by the municipal authorities.

Things start in their usual smoothness. Gustad is seen offering his "orisons to Ahura Mazda." (1) His son Sohrab gets admission to IIT, a symbol of pride. Gustad plans to celebrate it on the ninth birthday of Roshan, at which his very close friend Dinshawji is to be present. He brings a live chicken in the house, much to the embarrassment of his wife Dilnavaz. The initial atmosphere of gaiety, humour, songs, jokes and fun contributed by Dinshawji followed by a good dinner consisting of basmati rice, stew and chicken curry comes to an abrupt end when Sohrab turns violent uttering volleys of freakish remarks to his father and announcing that he is not going to join IIT and is not ready to part with his friends in the college and would pursue arts programme. The sudden and uncalled-for rebuff of Sohrab not only shatters all hopes of Gustad but also makes a surprising turn in the later course of the novel. It is from this point onward that there appears the theme of father-son hostility. Full of frustration when the table turns upside down, Gustad cannot hold his emotion in check:

> Throwing away his fortune without reason. What have I not done for him, tell me? I even threw myself in front of a car. Kicked him aside, saved his life, and got this to suffer all my life [slapping his hip]. But that's what a father is for. And if he cannot show respect at least, I can kick him again. Out of my home, out of my life! (52)

Eight years ago Gustad saved his son's life at the cost of his hip that fractured rendering him limp. True, as a loving father he did a lot for his son even buying almonds for Rs. 200 a Kg. to make him brainy. His shock and remorse are justified.

Once something is off the normal course others soon follow suit. Now many things start surfacing at an alarming rate. Soon Gustad has a row with Mr. Rabadi, another inmate of Khodadad building, over the latter's charge that Darius has an affair with his daughter. Gustad corners Mr. Rabadi, who is called by him "dogwalla," for his dog, Tiger, usually keeps deposits which are "copious and rather malodorous" (77) over Gustad's vinca and subjo bushes. Besides, Gustad is awaiting a letter from Major Bilimoria very anxiously which has not yet come. And he is disgusted at the horrid smell and flies and mosquitoes coming from the wall side that has been used as a public latrine: "The flies, the mosquitoes, the horrible stink, with bloody shameless people pissing, squatting alongside the wall. Late at night it became like a wholesale public latrine." (16) But the real event that poignantly changes and reverses Gustad's fortune is the coming of the long-awaited package from Bili-

moria. The package turns out to be a huge sum to the tune of ten lakh
rupees to be deposited in a bank in the name of one Mira Obili. The
whole thing makes both Gustad and Dilnavaz's hair stand erect, who do
not know how to hide such a huge amount. And even before the amount
is deposited, the secret of the money being received is smelt out by others. Gustad feels ill-at-ease when Tehmul tells the inspector that the former has a mountain of money in his flat. Another woman also makes a
reference to the money, to his utter dismay. The forbidden package thus
drives away Gustad's peace and happiness and he feels annoyed and betrayed. First he hides the money in the kitchen, and then with the help of
Dinshawji he deposits the whole amount in the bank since he is unable
to meet Ghulam Mohammad from whom he got the package. Taking
Dinshawji into confidence, he lets him know all about Major Bilimoria,
a RAW Officer, his letter and direct involvement in the training of
Mukti Bahinis against the Pakistan army. But the situation never improves. Amidst fear and restlessness on two consecutive days, Gustad
finds a headless bandicoot at the base of his vinca and again a headless
cat in the compound. Then a folded paper on which is written a nursery
rhyme in pencil is also found inserted between two adjacent branches of
his vinca bush. All these contribute to Gustad's unhappiness, landing
him in the dark land of suspicion. Futhermore, his daughter's suffering
from enervating diarrhoea occupies his mind. Then follows his quarrel
with Mr. Rabadi, the former asking Rabadi to train his dog, and the latter asking Gustad to teach his son manners and discipline.

However, the most disturbing is Dinshawji's inadvertent disclosure
to Laurie Coutino, a typist in the bank, where both Gustad and Dinshawji are working, of the whole secrecy impersonating himself as a
man working for secret service, and in charge of ten lakh rupees to fully
equip the Mukti Bahini guerrillas. Gustad sees the imminent danger
Dinshawji's frolicksome spree directly invites. When Dinshawji is taken
to task reminding him of the grave situation in which they are drawn he
(Dinshawji) writhes in the background, suddenly changing his character
from a man of public entertainer to a reserved person. Now whosoever
greets him gets a stock response from Dinshawji: "Thussook-thussook,
my cart rumbles along." (185) At times Gustad feels guilty of what really has happened to Dinshawji.

As things rush towards a climax, the arrest of Major Bilimoria on
charges of corruption is published in the paper. The heavens fall; Gustad's horizon is completely darkened with fear and uncertainty that his
complicity may be established. In the meantime Ghulam Mohammad
asks Gustad in a semi-threatening tone to return the whole amount in

one month's time to save Bilimoria's life. And to make things worse, Roshan's illness continues, and even the worst thing happens: she relapses. When Gustad visits Dr. Paymaster to report to him Roshan's continuous illness, he is taunted by the doctor who thinks that he has modified the prescription at will so that the illness assumes an unexpected proportion. Poverty haunts Gustad; he cannot make both ends meet, sells his camera and his wife's two gold marriage bangles. It is at this time that his rose plant, the vinca and subjo bush are hacked to the ground. Roshan's big doll in bridal array, which she received as the first prize in Annual School Raffle, is lost. It is at this critical juncture, again, that Dinshawji is hospitalized after a sudden collapse in the office. The first great blow in Gustad's life comes in the form of the death of Dinshawji, despite his prayer for the lives and recovery of both Roshan and Dinshawji at the Mount Mary. Shortly after that Gustad makes a trip to Delhi to meet Major Bilimoria who wants to tell him all that had happened. It is a big fraud of sixty lakh rupees in which Prime Minister gets directly involved. Bilimoria is asked to get the money from the SBI Director on an emergency basis to finance the guerrilla training pending official sanction by impersonating Prime Minister's voice on telephone. After that Major Bilimoria is asked to write a confession which he did without any second thought. But as soon as the money was received Prime Minister's office intercepted the money before it was used for the original purpose. Knowing the trick, Bilimoria kept ten lakh rupees for distribution to his friends. Before long he was arrested and kept under detention and tortured cruelly until he returned the money:

> On the bed lay nothing more than a shadow. The shadow of the powerful-built army man who once lived in Khodadad building. His hairline had receded, and sunken cheeks made the bones jut sharp and grotesque. The regal handlebar moustache was no more. His eyes had disappeared within their sockets. The neck . . . was as crany as poor *behesti* Dinshawji's, while under the sheet there seemed barely a trace of those strong shoulders and deep chest which Gustad and Dilnavaz used to point out as a good example to their sons, reminding them always to walk erect, with chest out and stomach in, like Major Uncle. (267)

Bilimoria gets four years' imprisonment, and while serving his term he dies of heart attack and his funeral at Tower of Silence takes place.

Things keep on taking their own course. Roshan's condition im-

proves and she is ready for her school. At least the family returned to
normal. Sohrab as usual pays his visit to his mother during the office
hour of his father. Mrs. Dilnavaz informs him about the death of Dinshawji, all about Ghulam Mohammad and the tragic death of Major Bilimoria. She implores Sohrab to stay and talk to his father nicely, who
would be coming in a short while from the funeral of Major Bilimoria.
Sohrab foresees a fight between him and his father because he knows he
is responsible for the latter's unhappiness. He reacts: "It's no use. I
spoilt all his dreams, he is not interested in me any more." (321) But the
mother rules out anything untoward would happen: "So much has happened since you left. Daddy has changed. It will be different now."
Gustad returns home at the time when the outer wall of Khodadad building, now converted into a holy wall with so many gods and goddesses
from all religions painted by a pavement artist at the request of Gustad
so that the area could be saved from pollution, from the horrid smell of
urine and excrement, and from the flies and mosquitoes bred there, is
about to be broken by a team of municipal workers under the command
of Malcolm Saldanha. The destruction is, however, checked by a morcha jointly formed by people from all walks of life ranging from doctor
to prostitutes to snake charmers and paanwallas. Soon an exchange of
angry words ensues, and morcha's insistence that the wall be kept intact
is not listened to by the municipal workers who proceed with a go-ahead
signal from the authority. The heated debate culminates in stone throwing. Excited at the sight of the flying missiles, Tehmul Lungraa goes out
and is targetted and falls flat with a broken forehead and succumbs to
the injury instantly. Taking the dead body inside the room of Tehmul,
Gustad prays reciting the Yatha Ahu Varyo five times and Ashem Vahoo three times with tears shedding from his eyes.

At this significant moment, Gustad comes out of himself to be one
with death and one with life. He prays for all, cries for all, for him, for
Tehmul, for Jimmy, for Dinshawji, for his papa and mama, for grandpa
and grandma, "all who had to wait for so long." (337) He prays for the
mercy of God on all souls, for the end is come, maybe to start again
from the beginning. Out of this vast vacuum, there emerges a profound
meaning that signifies the archetypal cycle of birth, death and rebirth
motifs. It is at this moment that he accepts the return of his prodigal son,
who comes to him. It is in complete surrender that the father and the son
lose their personalities and exercise their hatred of each other. Now they
reach out to each other:

Gustad turned around. He saw his son standing in the doorway, and each held the other's eyes. Still he sat, gazing upon his son, and Sohrab waited motionless in the doorway, till at last Gustad got to his feet slowly. Then he went up and put his arms around him. 'Yes,' said Gustad running his bloodstained fingers once through Sohrab's hair. 'Yes,' he said, 'yes,' and hugged him tightly once more. (337)

The novel, while representing this larger rhythm with universal significance, tries to bring in other smaller rhythms within its fold. One notices alongside the main plot there runs a sub-plot to effect the return of Sohrab and cure the illness of Roshan through magico-religious rites performed by Mrs. Dilnavaz following the advice of Miss Kutpitia. Miss Kutpitia is a person who "wanted to offer help and advice on matters unexplainable by the laws of nature. She claimed to know about curses and spells: both to cast and remove; about magic: black and white; about omens and auguries; about dreams and their interpretation. Most important of all . . . was the ability to understand the hidden meaning of mundane events and chance occurrences; and her fanciful, fantastical imagination could be entertaining at times." (4) Dilnavaz becomes so unnerved when her husband and Sohrab carry on fighting, abusing each other very frequently, as her son loses interest in IIT, till at last he leaves her house in violent protest against his father's anger and threat unleashed against him. Equally disturbing is the illness of her daughter, Roshan, that goes on worsening day by day.

In fact, the misfortune that befalls Gustad's family is interpreted by Miss Kutpitia from her own ideological point of view rooted in beliefs and superstitions, culturally accepted and transmitted from generation to generation. First, the genesis of the trouble in Dilnavaz's family is attributed to the killing of a live bird in the house—the live chicken brought by Gustad to celebrate his son's selection to IIT and the birthday of Roshan. Killing a bird in the house is very ominous, according to Miss Kutpitia. Second, what has happened at the dinner party has many things to do with the incident which took place at Miss Kutpitia's home the same day. In the morning Miss Kutpitia had killed a lizard on her breakfast table, its broken tail wriggling and dancing for about five minutes, a definite omen forbidding her to go out for the next twenty-four hours. She declines therefore the honour of joining the dinner party. The ominous incident also casts its spell over the dinner party. The initial gusto and merriment of the party decelerate and sink into much sound and fury when Gustad and Sohrab tone up their differences, anger and arguments with the unwarranted declaration by Sohrab that he is no

longer interested in IIT. Light also went off a short while ago much to
the displeasure of all. Darkness symbolizes the eclipse of the father-son
relationship. Nobody feels like eating, and the whole effort and relish go
unappreciated: "Of the nine chicken portions, six remained in the dish."
(50) When the matter is brought to the notice of Miss Kutpitia by the
apparently worried mother, the former attributes all this to *"jaadu-man-
tar."* (63) She further contends that somebody tries to gain the interest
of Sohrab out of his own loss of interest and that there are ways and
means to set things right. Dilnavaz is instructed to do some magic rites
for a few days before the setting of the sun. In this process the trial goes
on, but the result is far from being satisfactory. Sohrab drinks some lime
juice prepared by his mother who does some magic to regain her son's
lost interest. But this comes to no avail. Now somebody has to drink a
juice mixed with lime juice to transfer the spell from Sohrab to the second person. Both choose Tehmul to be the target. Still there is little effect on Sohrab's mind. Instead things go from bad to worse: Sohrab revolts and leaves home and Roshan's illness becomes a matter of great
concern. Miss Kutpitia maintains that Roshan's illness is caused by evil
eye. To protect her from it, she asks Dilnavaz to perform a ritual:

> Take your needle and thread, a nice strong thread with a big knot
> at the end. Select a yellow lime, and seven chillies. Chillies must
> be green, not turning red. Never red. String them together with the
> needle. Lime goes at the bottom. Then hang the whole thing over
> your door, inside the house. (149-50)

Then she goes on, "It is like a *taveej*, a protection. Each time Roshan
walks under it, the evil eye becomes less and less powerful. Actually . . .
everyone in your family will benefit." (150) But even this does not
relieve Roshan of her illness. It is both evil eye and some dark force that
are responsible for the continuous illness, argues Miss Kutpitia.
Ultimately, she discovers and makes Dilnavaz see that the person
behind is a man who has a dog, suggesting that Mr. Rabadi is the man.
As regards Sohrab's not coming home, Miss Kutpitia asks Dilnavaz to
get some nails of Tehmul to burn in coal fire. And when the nails are
melted, then turmeric and cayenne powders are to be sprinkled. This
ritual "would open wide Tehmul's channels . . . through which his spirit
would reach and yank the evil out of Sohrab's brain." (153) Even that
helps little. So the last remedy is thought out: that is lizard ritual, amidst
Miss Kutpitia's warning: "Terrible things could happen. And not all
your sorrow or regret later on will do any good, or change one single

thing." (275) Some miracle or coincidence does take place: Roshan gets better; Gustad returns home safely from a trip to Delhi; and even Sohrab's absence, Dilnavaz thinks, "would now somehow be put right." (292) Whether the return of Sohrab has something to do with the death of Tehmul is yet a matter of speculation. Surprisingly, the day Sohrab changes his mind, Tehmul dies. All this seems to correspond with the dire consequence Miss Kutpitia had warned Dilnavaz of. But things at this level remain highly unexplainable.

Whether one believes in God or not, throughout the novel there are anecdotes related to gods and goddesses, and miracles like that of St. Thomas who landed on the Malabar coast amongst the fishermen nineteen hundred years ago and who spread Christianity among the Hindus, Brahmins, Sadhus and Acharyas. (24-25) The Mount Mary and St. Haji Ali episodes are equally breath-taking. One of the most important things Mistry wants to emphasize is religious tolerance on the basis that all religions are equal. The pavement artist, who has painted gods and goddesses from all religions of the world on the wall, is one through whom the Indian secularism is reinforced. The morcha director shouts: "The wall of Hindu and Muslim, Sikh and Christian, Parsi and Buddhist! A holy wall, a wall suitable for worship and devotion, whatever your faith!" (326) Mistry's concept of faith cannot be questioned. About faith he makes the pavement artist speak thus:

> You see, I don't like to weaken anyone's faith. Miracle, magic, mechanical trick, coincidence—does it matter what it is, as long as it helps? Why analyse the strength of the imagination, the power of suggestion, power of auto-suggestion, the potency of psychological pressures? Looking too closely is destructive, makes everything disintegrate. As it is, life is difficult enough. Why to simply make it tougher? After all, who is to say what makes a miracle and what makes a coincidence? (289)

The sub-plot woven around Kutpitia-Dilnavaz also reaffirms this conviction. This theme that seemingly goes out of proportion may look like something disjointed or mechanical in the total structure of the novel like the Clarissa and Septimus parts in *Mrs. Dalloway* at the first glance. But at a closer look, its structural function cannot be ruled out because it is this thematic development by way of a sub-plot that integrates the novel's central disintegrating and conflicting human elements. It is Dilnavaz and not Gustad who tries to make Sohrab come to terms with his father. It is ultimately her triumph that brings order in

the midst of chaos. Gustad's epic struggle against a hostile and
indifferent world would not have had a profound meaning without the
final reconciliation. When Dilnavaz comes out with the benign qualities
of a mother in these words, '"He is your father. He will always love you
and want the best for you,'" (321) the barrier between the father and the
son gives way and dissolves.

Though Mistry is highly imbued with an original wirter's imagination in the development of a flawless story in *Such a Long Journey*, his
awareness of the contemporary social and political situation of India,
particularly the period of the 1971 Indo-Pak war, is extremely exciting.
As a realist, he wields the weapon of satire, which makes him a ruthless
artist, a stern political satirist and a devout critic of war. His attack on
Nehru and Indira Gandhi is unprecedented. Describing the humiliating
defeat of India at the hands of the Chinese in the Indo-Chinese war of
1962, he does not spare even Nehru for fighting a war of defeat, a "humiliating defeat." (9) Mistry goes on describing Nehru's frustration, ill
temper, political intrigues that surrounded him, his feud with Feroze
Gandhi for the latter's exposure of scandals in the Government, his obsession with his "darling daughter Indira," who left her husband in order to live with him, whose "monomaniacal fixation occupied his days
and nights." (11) He praises, however, Lal Bahadur Shastri, who became India's Prime Minister upon the death of Nehru, because with his
rule "the stagnant waters of government would at last be freshened and
vitalized." (114) Shastri could do in the Indo-Pak war of 1965 far better
than what Nehru did in the war with China. Dr. Paymaster rightly says
of him: "Short in height but tall in brains is our Lal Bahadur." (114) In
this sudden death at Tashkent, beside the possibility of a Pakistani or
Russian plot, the role of Indira Gandhi is suspected: "so that her father's dynastic democratic dream could finally come true." (114) There
are direct attacks on Indira Gandhi for her nationalization of banks, for
her encouragement to make a separate Maharashtra state that caused
bloodshed and riot, and for her creation of Shiv Sena to divide people
on class basis, as Dinshawji remarks, "wanting to make the rest of us
into second class citizens," (39) and for her narrow political gains, i.e.
to get votes of the poor by showing that she is on the side of the poor.
Her financing of her son's Maruti car manufacture, the secret Swiss
bank accounts, the use of RAW as her private police force to spy on her
political opponents and even on her own cabinet ministers, her involvement in sixty-lakh-rupees scandal, the very calculative move to save
herself at the cost of Major Bilimoria expose the decaying political order of Indian democracy. For a radical change, two things are suggested

by Sohrab as he puts what Major Bilimoria used to say: "'Only two choices: communism and military dictatorship, if you want to get rid of these Congress party crooks. Forget democracy for a few years, not meant for a starving country.'" (68) The nauseating dirt, ugliness and pollution in the city, in the bazaar, and at Khodadad building are a microcosm of what happens at the Centre. Congress party—for that matter, Congress Government,—"are called a rogues' gallery." (325) All people, men, women, grown ups, cannot tolerate decay, greed, treachery, dishonesty, fraud, moral turpitude and deception at the Centre. Dr. Paymaster puts the gravity of the situation metaphorically in the following terms:

> . . . our beloved country is a patient with gangrene at an advanced stage. Dressing the wound or sprinkling rosewater over it to hide the stink of rotting tissue is useless. Fine words and promises will not cure the patient. The decaying part must be excised. You see, the municipal corruption is merely the bad smell, which will disappear as soon as the gangrenous government at the centre is removed. (313)

The fictional world Mistry creates in *Such a Long Journey* is thus no utopia of any kind. It is a picture of the fallen world in which the call of the Holy Word is not heard. Again, it is a world in which all forms of corruption, knavery, hypocrisy, tyranny, ugliness and decay, have become the order of the day. The society which is depicted is completely deprived of resilience. Mistry's shock at the sight of stinking human condition and rampant corruption turns him into being a realist, who is obliged to expose the world around him. At times he looks like a naturalist reporting the human condition as in itself it is. Wars between nations, the complete lack of commitment on the part of the big powers, and so on show the degenerating political scenario in the international politics. The nationalistic fervour in the novelist makes him at times a ruthless critic of the corrupt government at the Centre. His nationalism is above petty selfishness. He keeps aside such things as turning up and selling of clothes and gold ornaments collected by way of donation during the Indo-Chinese war by politicians and fund-raisers in Chor Bazaar and Nul Bazaar without attaching much importance (though the satiric implication is deeply felt) as long as "the glow of national unity was still warm and comforting." (10) Though he is in favour of certain change, he cannot think of a political situation under dictatorship and communism. This is shown when Gustad snaps at his son, Sohrab, who speaks of dictatorship or communism as a better alternative to democracy: "Be grateful this is democracy. If that Russiawala was here, he would pack you and your friends off to Siberia." (69)

So when looked at closely, Rohinton Mistry is not a political anarchist, nor does he favour the blueprint of a new society based on radical change. But the most important thing, politics apart, that the novelist wants to emphasize is the question of life, i.e. the problem of human loneliness in the modern world. Gustad's sufferings and struggle with fortitude and humility in life re-echo the classical tragic hero's life and sufferings. The world Gustad is doomed to live in is, like Hamlet's Elsinore, torn by a time which is "out of joint." His quotation from Firdausi's *Shah-Nama* well conveys this state of the world: "How did they hold the world in the beginning, and why is it that it has been left to us in such a sorry state? And how was it that they were able to live free of care during the days of their heroic labours?" It is in this atmosphere that life has to get going. On the one hand, the journey from Firdausi's *Shah-Nama* to Tagore's *Gitanjali* (from which he also quotes) proves to be a long journey in a cold and hostile world. Gustad's friends, Dinshawji, Bilimoria and Tehmul, have already undertaken such a long journey, on the other, it is also a journey, a long journey, from hopelessness to hope, and from despondency to millennium. For Gustad the hard times are over, no matter how badly he has been battered.

To conclude, in *Such a Long Journey,* Rohinton Mistry comes out as a critical realist so far as the treatment of social reality is concerned. Through this method, his ideology comes out to project the kind of society he wants to be a part of. In his consciousness of the social and political aspects of a particular historical period he emerges as a progressive writer, but in his vision of a larger rhythm of life, in which all forms of human happiness and misery are seen woven inseparably in the development of the central character towards a climax, he shows his allegiance to literature's timeless values, independent of narrow commitments, whether political or regional. The novelist's departure from the emphasis on the representation of the psychic being of the character reveals the inadequacy of the novel-form in the post-modernist period. His interests in the predicament of modern life, the diseased effect of degenerating society on life, issue forth gushing in the novel. *Such a Long Journey* is a successful work of art in which crowd a variety of values generating a classical structure par excellence.

NOTE

1.   Rohinton Mistry, *Such a Long Journey* (New Delhi: Rupa, 1991).

Thematic Concerns in *Such a Long Journey*

ANITA MYLES

The Moving Finger writes; and having writ
Moves on, nor all thy Piety nor Wit
Shall lure it back to cancel half a line,
Nor all the tears wash out a Word of it.

T hese lines of Omar Khayyam remind one of one's utter helplessness at the callous hands of Destiny. The ancient Hindu and Greek mythologies have re-stated this fact in varied terms and writers through the ages have, in one way or the other, picked up the thread. Going through Rohinton Mistry's first attempt at fiction writing, *Such a Long Journey*, a serious reader will at once be struck by a note of re-interpretation of the same principle of Fate which is so vividly manifested in the lines by the eminent Persian poet.

Published in 1991, Mistry's novel appears to be a descriptive story of a few middle-class characters in the contemporary modern set up. However, hidden behind an apparently simple narrative are manifold attempts to give a new orientation to certain basic and serious issues of life.

It is interesting to note that the title of the novel has been taken from T.S. Eliot's "The Journey of the Magi":

A cold coming we had of it,
Just the worst time of the year
For a journey, and such a long journey. . . .[1]

The title has a symbolic significance and refers to the life of Dr. Gustad Noble, the central character of the story. Gustad was a teller in a bank. As an ordinary man, he had to face many trials in life. But he had his own dreams about the future. He also had plans for his eldest son, Sohrab. But one by one the aspirations crumble down like a pack of cards. Traditional family ties are witnessed loosening. The reticent attitude of his wife, Dilnavaz, is explicit when she re-assuringly says to him, "We must be patient." However, Gustad has borne this far too long and it seems that his patience has been tested to the last string: "What have we been all these years if not patient? Is this how it will end? Sorrow, nothing but sorrow."[2] The family gets more and more involved in suffering as Darius, the second son, falls in love with Mr. Rabadi's daughter and Roshan, the daughter, keeps ill health. Yet all these do not deter Gustad from facing life stoically.

Fortunately, Gustad Noble had a few good and understanding friends like Major Jimmy Bilimoria and Dinshawji, the latter working with him in the bank. One day Jimmy suddenly left Khodadad Building, where he lived, without a word even to Gustad, which upset the latter. He was already disillusioned with the indifferent behaviour of Sohrab and now the disappearance of a close friend made matters worse. After some time, Gustad gets a letter from Jimmy, who desired Gustad to receive a parcel from him. Gustad readily does so in the name of friendship. However, on opening the parcel, he finds himself entrapped in an intricate and apparently inextricable snare of difficulties.

The parcel contains ten lakh rupees to be deposited in the bank in an account held under the name of a non-existent woman, Mira Obili. Gustad takes the help of Dinshawji for accomplishing this task. As soon as the work is done Jimmy wants the money back. This is another uphill task. Then Gustad has to go to New Delhi to see the ailing Jimmy. Gustad feels utterly lonely and lost as two of his friends depart from this world one after the other, first it is Dinshawji and then Jimmy.

As the years roll by Gustad Noble modifies his dreams and trims his expectations in life. Experience makes him into a stronger, more enduring man. He firmly resolves to face life stoicallly and not to be crushed by the forces of destiny. This attitude is his greatest triumph in life.

Rohinton Mistry, as mentioned earlier, is indebted to Eliot's "The Journey of the Magi" for the title of this novel. Eliot's poem is highly symbolic. The journey of the three wise men to the birthplace of Jesus Christ is not merely an ordinary physical journey; it is symbolic of man's spiritual quest in which he has to undergo numerous hardships. Later, one of the Magi gives an account of his toilsome journey for the benefit of a listener. He distinctly reveals how he was impelled to proceed merely beause of his faith. He succeeded in overcoming all the impediments that befell his way. The end of the journey was rewarding and satisfying, for he had reached his destination and found that the prophecy of the birth of Christ was true. The journey of the Magi is also symbolic of the re-orientation which is absolutely essential to attain higher and nobler values in life.

Gustad's journey of life is so close to the journey of the Magi. Gustad was keenly desirous of the fulfilment of his dreams and aspirations. At every stage of his life's journey, he met with unprecedented obstacles and the working of inexplicable forces. However, he is not the one to give in; he is like the wise man who very subtly pushed aside the hindrances of life, did not allow them to overpower him and went ahead with faith that the journey will surely end at a particular destination.

The variegated experiences of life help Gustad to come to a very significant conclusion: "Luck is the spit of the Gods and Goddesses." (338) Though the novelist has made a pavement artist utter this thought, yet it is in its totality appropriately applicable to the life of Gustad. He never shunned the problems of life; nor was he in any way mortified by his experiences. As he himself says, "it was his strength of spirit" which made the journey possible. He purposefully made himself tough so much so that he did not shed even a single tear on the death of his mother. But after all Gustad was humane and when his steadfastness was tested by the betrayal of Sohrab and Jimmy Bilimoria he breaks down saying: "I don't understand this world anymore . . . what a world of wickedness it has become!" (142) Mistry's ideas about destiny are akin to those of Thomas Hardy, who wrote in his poem "To Life":

> O, life with the sad sacred face
> I weary, of seeing thee,
> I know what thou wouldst tell
> Of Death, Time, Destiny—
> I have known it long, and know, too well,
> What it all means for me.

Hardy opines that man is bound to the wheel of destiny and therefore has to continuously struggle against the decrees of fate. This in no way means that man should surrender meekly. The Greeks also believed that the Malignant Power and the Immanent Will stand firmly against the plans of the frail and feeble creature called man. William Shakespeare reiterates the same view in *King Lear*:

> As flies to wanton boys, are we to the Gods
> They kill us for their sport.

Significantly enough, Mistry's message is not that of a cynic or a pessimist; rather it is that of a meliorist, who believes that the individual must accept what destiny has in store for him.

The novelist has created the character of the pavement artist to communicate to the readers his own views about God, Man and Destiny. The artist paints pictures of Gods representing different religions. He gives these Gods a variety of facial expressions by means of his brush:

> The holy countenances on the wall—some grim and vengeful, some jovial, some compassionate, others frightful and awe-inspiring, yet others kind and avuncular—watch over the road, the traffic, the passers-by, day and night. (184)

The variegated countenances of God are symbolic and for each man God has a different image. Some may be pleased with the blessings of God while others may curse him for their sufferings. The artist seems to utter the message of the novelist that man must carry on whatever may come his way:

> Over the years, a precise cycle had entered the rhythm of his life, the cycle of arrival, creation and obliteration. Like sleeping, waking and stretching, or eating, digesting and excreting, the cycle sang in harmony with the blood in his veins and the breath in his lungs. He learned to disdain the overlong sojourn and the procrastinated departure, for they were the progenitors of the complacent routine, to be shunned at all costs. The journey—chanced, unplanned, solitary—was the thing to relish. (184)

Mistry also emphasizes the role of chance. In his opinion, life should be treated as a gift from God, and even if it is full to the brim with misery and misfortune, it 'ought to be relished and lived to the lees. It is true that men become 'confused and discontented' as they await 'the uncertain future.'

Hope is a powerful anchor for the troubled mind. Man attempts to solve his problems by wishing for miracles to happen, though many times miracles and misfortunes come simultaneously. During the course of the story Mistry mentions that when people are desperate, their prayers seem to go unheard, the future seems to be bleak and there appears to be no alternative, then they resort to exorcism. Coincidentally, it works and at least for the time being things seems to be set right. The novelist writes:

> Miracle, magic, mechanical trick, coincidence—does it matter

what it is, as long as it helps? why analyse the strength of the
imagination, the power of suggestion, potency of psychological
pressures? Looking too closely is destructive, makes everything
disintegrate. As it is, life is difficult enough. Why to simply make
it tougher? After all, who is to say what makes a miracle and what
makes a coincidence? (289)

The wall on which the pavement artist works so diligently represents the
oneness of all religions. There is one common factor in all the religions
of the world—the faith of the worshippers. God chooses novel methods
to test man's faith. Mistry puts Gustad through numerous episodes in
the novel, all of which point to the inevitable fact that the Hand of
Providence is supreme.

The novelist shows the supremacy of the Divine Power by creating
the character of Tehmul, Gustad's neighbour. While describing the
death of Tehmul, the novelist writes: "Tehmul dropped without a sound,
his figure folding gracefully. The dance is over." (333) In this context
the word 'dance' becomes meaningful, for it symbolizes man's helplessness at the hands of relentless destiny. God, the potter, shapes the human vessel according to his own design, and the 'clay pot' shatters into
pieces when the Master Puppeteer chooses to end the 'dance' of life.
This interpretation is not precisely cynical or pessimistic but it reveals
the basic progression of the story, which seems to convey that the human actor must have a resigned attitude because he is subjugated to the
Immanent Will.

In the context of Tehmul's death, the word 'dance,' if interpreted on
the basis of Hindu mythology, signifies a highly pragmatic attitude to
life. Tehmul sacrificed his life for a good cause. He was one of the
throng that protested to save the 'holy' wall symbolizing unity. One of
the Trinity (Trimurti), Lord Shiva is believed to be the symbol of death
and destruction. His 'Tandava Nritya' shakes the very foundation of human existence. Nevertheless, at the highest pitch of his rhythmic movement the 'Nritya' takes up a circular shape, which signifies the continuous process of life and death. So, according to the Hindu system of belief, death is certainly not an end in itself. It is the hopeful foundation of
a rebirth, and by his noble deeds a man may be reborn in a better situation in life. The mentally-retarded Tehmul dies a noble death of sacri-
fice and, therefore, may be reborn as a normal human being. Actually,
the entire life of Tehmul has been an unwilling dance to the tunes of the
Master Puppeteer. Born a normal human being, Tehmul becomes men-
tally incapacitated due to an accident early in life. He leads a life of de-

rision, mockery and fun. But now that he dances to the final tune, he has achieved the ultimate truth of life in death.

There is an ironic ambivalence in Rohinton Mistry's delineation of the character of Dinshawji. He did not have a very smooth going with his wife, whom he often referred to as 'domestic vulture.' His health, too, was steadily deteriorating. Yet Dinshawji never allowed his sufferings to surface to the foreground. In fact, they were neatly camouflaged under the mask of his jovial temperament. His licentious way of joking with Laurie Coutino, an office worker, landed him in trouble. Gustad came to his assistance and advised him thus:

> What you must do is stop your jokes and teasing with everyone. At the same time, I will start telling people that poor Dinshawji's health is not good again, he is feeling completely under the weather. (180)

This bit of sane advice sounded like a death knell for Dinshawji, who from the very next day conjured up and projected his new image of "the grave individual, suddenly fragile and spent." The so far indomitable Dinshawji is now different. He is compromised to destiny because he is as human as any one else, as much a puppet in the hands of 'Destiny' as the others are. Gustad stands guilty of "confiscating his mask." In depicting this humorous, gay and light-hearted character, Mistry has adeptly synthesized the myth and reality, the humour and pathos of human existence.

In his first novel, Rohinton Mistry emerges as a realist. He has made use of two contrivances for this purpose—one is the plot, and the other is the language and style. Mistry has portrayed the life of an ordinary middle-class man who has to live a life beset with problems. The plot is based on the personal experiences and observations of the novelist. Rohinton Mistry was born in Bombay, and in 1975 he went to Toronto, where he worked in a bank for ten years. Thus he preferred to make the central character of his first novel a bank worker and has given the story the locale of the metropolis of Bombay.

The language used in the novel is a fine specimen of Indian English and at once reminds the reader of the language of Mulk Raj Anand, which is termed as 'Mulkese' by Khushwant Singh. Following the same pattern, Mistry makes use of Hindi words. Some abuses have been translated into English. Perhaps this is necessitated by the novelist's spontaneity of expression. Some of the words which are frequently used in quotidian life recur in the novel. Some examples are: *bhaiya, yaar,*

humko kuch nahin maloom, masala, bismillah, gaswalla, chalo, morcha,
chowki, theek hai, bay-sharam, parinaam, etc. At one or two places
there is a literal translation of Hindi phrases. He writes of the cowardly
manner in which some soldiers left the front and ran away—"turned tail
and ran." In addition, he uses four-letter words profusely.

However, this in no way means that Mistry is incapable of using
polished and refined language. There are several passages in the novel
which flawlessly express the writer's point of view. Mistry emerges as a
true Indian writer, for the scenes, the situation, the characters and even
the language reflect the typical Indian culture vividly.

Mistry has incorporated some ancient myths from the Persian, the
Hindu, the Greek and the Christian sources related to several perennial
truths in order to depict the plight of the modern man. The human protagonist, as revealed by the novelist, is perpetually involved in an unequal conflict with the supernal forces which are beyond his control, but
he does not submit. One must not be misled to believe, however, that
Mistry was directly influenced by any of the above-mentioned myths. In
this sense he is in line with Shakespeare and Hardy, who have examined
the human conditions for a contemporary commentary on life and have
projected this condition into the future. Such writers are bound to carve
a niche for themselves.

The novel deals with the Parsis, and certain customs and rituals related to the community are graphically described, as is clear from the
account of the ceremonies related to the last rites. Of course, this is
nothing unexpected in a novelist who himself is a Parsi. The entire
novel is steeped in Indian sensibility. Eminent Indian critics and schol-
ars like C.D. Narasimhaiah, M.K. Naik and K.R.S. Iyengar have frequently maintained that if Indian writing in English has to survive the
test of time and also to maintain its recognition *vis-a-vis* other Commonwealth literatures cropping up in English so profusely, then more than
the medium, emphasis must be on maintaining a certain standard of Indian sensibility.

Such a Long Journey views and reviews a vast canvas of Indian life.
It discusses minutely and realistically the ups and downs of an average
Indian and also touches certain explosive chapters of the Indian politics
and the three wars that took place between 1962 and 1971.

It is too early to state definitely whether Rohinton Mistry would
transcend time as a creative writer, but the re-orientation of myths
which he has successfully moulded to suit his design in this novel promises a bright future for him.

NOTES

1. *The Complete Poems and Plays of T.S. Eliot* (London: Faber and Faber, 1982), p. 103.
2. *Such a Long Journey* (New Delhi: Rupa, 1991), p. 52.

The Parsi Community in
Such a Long Journey

JAYDIPSINH DODIYA

There are a few novelists like Rohinton Mistry whose works centralize their community. This is especially true of immigrant writers from the minority communities. For instance in M.G. Vassanji's novels *The Gunny Sack* and *No New Land*, it is the odyssey of his Khoja community in particular and that of Asian community in general. Similarly, Firdaus Kanga in his *Trying to Grow*, Farrukh Dhondy in *Bombay Duck*, Bapsi Sidhwa in *The Crow Eaters* and *The Pakistani Bride* reflect Parsi community in diverse hues. Their works exhibit consciousness of their community in a way that the community emerges as a protagonist relegating human protagonists to the background.

The Parsis migrated from Iran to the west coast of India to escape religious persecution in the eighth century. They were permitted by local rulers to stay and practise their faith. In spite of being an infinitesimal minority they have contributed much to the development of India. Though they are one of the world, they do possess a sort of ability to laugh at the cruel complexities of life. The Parsi writers are also sensitive to the various anxieties felt by their community.

Rohinton Mistry has demonstrated this in responding to the existing threats to the Parsi family and community, and also to the country. He presents his community through the different narratives of his characters who invariably express their concern for their community and the changes that affect their community. Since their fate is bound up with the fate of their community, their stories tend to be the stories of their community. By centralizing their community in their narratives, they preserve and protect themselves and thus they throw light on the existing facts.

After the great Parsi exodus to the west coast of India in the eighth century, a few Zoroastrians continued to live in secrecy in the hills, caves and forests of Iran. The rest of the Persian population wasforciblyconvertedtoIslam.

The Parsi community is on a long journey to growing and knowing in Mistry's *Such a Long Journey* written somewhat in the manner of fiction or non-fiction. *Such a Long Journey* is set in Bombay against the backdrop of war in the Indian subcontinent and the birth of Bangladesh. The novel tells the story of Dr. Gustad Noble, an ordinary man, and the peculiar way in which the conflict impinges on the lives of his family.

Gustad Noble's dreams and aspirations are quite modest, and when circumstances conspire to deny him even these modest expectations, he finds it hard to accept that he cannot make things happen the way he wants them to. As the novel unfolds, he discovers that there are other forces at play, larger than him and mostly inexplicable, so being the trials of Gustad Noble, loss of a dear friendship, the son's betrayal of his father's dream, the illness of Gustad's daughter, his friend Dinshawji's death. As Gustad Noble slowly modifies his dreams and trims down his expectations of life, he comes to accept that he is not in control of events. His triumph consists in his manner of enduring these trials.

For Gustad there is no God who appears at the end of his tribulations to explain things or to dispense justice, no God to reassure him that he has passed the test and that all will be well. And yet Gustad survives without succumbing to any prolonged despair or bitterness, still in possession of his essential human dignity.

Such a Long Journey is a brilliant first novel by one of the most remarkable writers to have emerged from the Indian literary tradition in many years. In this novel Dinshwaji remarks: "What days those were, Yaar. What fun we used to have. Parsees were the kings of banking in those days. Such respect we used to get. Now the whole atmosphere has been spoiled ever since that Indira nationalized the banks."

Gustad too adds: "Nowhere in the world has nationalization worked." What can you say to idiots? Like Gustad other members of the community are scared of politicians like Mrs. Gandhi whom they consider responsible for encouraging the demand for a separate Maharashtra: "How much bloodshed, how much rioting she caused." (39) As a minority community, the Parsis have their little fears and anxieties. Dinshawji voices his concern about rising communal forces: "No future for minorities, with all these Shiv Sena politics and Marathi language nonsense. It was going to be like the black people in America twice as good as the white men to get half as much. How could he make Sohrab understand this?" (55)

In *Such a Long Journey,* various characters belonging to the minority community express their anguish at the changing pattern of communal relationship in a society that breathes beneath the narrative structure of the novel.

Rohinton Mistry's sensitivity of impending dangers to his community is expressed by his characters' consciousness of these changes. In a nutshell, Mistry's *Such a Long Journey* centralizes the Parsi community in many ways.

Novel as History: A Study of
Such a Long Journey and *A Fine Balance*

NILA SHAH

T he term history, in the narrow sense, is the science of the human past. In the wider sense, it studies the development of the earth, of the heavens and of species, as well as of civilization.[1] It is often used to designate the sum total of human activities in the past. A more common usage looks upon history as the record of the event rather than the events themselves. In this latter and objective sense, history is "all we know about everything man has ever done or thought or hoped or felt."[2] However if subjectively contemplated, history may be regarded as a record of all that has occurred within the realm of human consciousness.[3]

Although the origin of the history can be traced back to the oldest documents of 'Eolithic' or 'paleolithic' ages, the historiography did not come into existence until the art of writing had been mastered. The earliest historical material or inscriptions were devoted chiefly to glorification of the kings, military victories and monarchian achievements. Consequently history was reduced to dynastic lists. More often than not, myths, folk-tales and panegyric songs pre-occupied the so-called historians of ancient time.

In recent times, however, new historicists have challenged the traditional concept of history as casual, closed and linear. Theorists like Foucault and Hayden White opine that since history, when made up by the historian, is necessarily a political act, the empirical and objective narration of historical material should be discarded as 'real' life can never be truthfully represented.[4] Friedrich Nietzsche writes: "the historical sense in our time forms a sixth sense, prevading the philosophy, history and culture of modern era."[5] Ezra Pound says: "our knowledge of the past is marred by 'omissions' of the most vital facts."[6] Historiography, in fact, is a poetic construct and the historian has to interpret his materials in order to construct the moving pattern of images in which the form of the historical process is to be mirrored.[7] And the historian must 'interpret' his data by either excluding certain facts from his account as irrelevant to his narrative purpose or in order to reconstruct, he must include in his narrative an account of some events for which the facts regarding the explanation of its occurrence are lacking. In either case, the historian 'interprets' his material by filling in the gaps in his information on inferential or speculative grounds. In this way, to borrow Droysen's words, "the historical records are incomplete."[8] That leads to an argument that if we can say with some certitude "what happened," we cannot always say, on the basis of the record "why" it happened as it did. The writer of historical narrative on the other hand brings with him a notion of the 'story' that lies embedded in the "facts" given by the record. In fact there are infinite such stories contained therein, all different in their details, each unlike every other.

Novels, on the other hand, tend to present an intimate view of life while providing a holistic picture of perceived reality. They transport the reader into a particular setting to involve him/her in the lives and thoughts of a set of characters. The development of these fictitious characters, however, occur against a background of their socio-political environs. The writers in general and the postcolonial writers in particular endeavour to postulate their own version of history of their people, and thereby reject the traditional history. Hence, a novelist shares 'emplotting strategies' with an historian who excludes, emphasizes or subordinates details of historical events.

A postcolonial writer who has inherited the same emplotting strategies rejects the preceding stories about his people and weaves his own. The change that matters comes in the postcolonial narrator's viewpoint. Rohinton Mistry, too, in his novels *Such a Long Journey* (1991) and *A Fine Balance* (1995) rejects many existing narratives about post-Independence historical happenings and achieves a fusion between fact and fiction.

Such a Long Journey deals with its protagonist, Gustad Noble's modest dreams and aspirations. The novelist has dovetailed various narratives with the central narrative of Gustad. The novel is set in Mumbai, depicting life-style of Parsis in the city. However, it is not about an ordinary man and his family. The novelist is more concerned about narration of some of the major events of the history of post-independent India. Mistry has competently deployed the feelings and apprehensions of a minority community to ascertain some of the historical events. The life-style of Parsis living in Khodadad Building is the microcosm of the Parsis in India, Mistry has exploited history to probe into broader concerns of Parsis and of national identity with fate and war as two major themes of the novel. He has taken much pain to reflect on these themes at personal, social and national levels.

Though the novel seems extremely simple in its structure, history of a community and that of a certain period of a country pulsates within the story. Mistry's narration like that of Peerbhoy Paanwalla's titillating tales is not "tragedy, comedy or history; not pastoral, tragical-comical, historical-pastoral or tragical-historical . . . it possessed a smattering of all these characteristics."[9]

At one level Gustad's fate resembles fate of a nation. India, like Gustad—confronted with wars and the aftermath—is under trauma, and limps awkwardly. On the other level, the writer's concern for his community is depicted through various characters. The novel recounts the journey of Parsis who came to this land all the way from Iran in the 7th century A.D. Gustad is proud of his ancient roots when talking to Malcolm, "but our prophet Zarathustra lived more than fifteen hundred years before your Son of God was ever born." (24) Various characters belonging to Parsi community bring to the fore peculiar traits of their community. More often than not, together with their traditions, fears and anxieties are the focal points. For instance, Gustad voices his concerns, "No future for minorities, with all these fascist Shiv Sena politics and Marathi language nonsense." (55) Dinshawji thinks that Parsis are impaired, "what days those were, yaar. . . . Parsis were the kings of banking in those days. . . . Ever since that Indira nationalized the banks." (38) He also abuses her for disharmony in Maharashtra, "At once she began encouraging the demands for a separate Maharashtra. How much bloodshed, how much rioting she caused." (39) Besides this, the frequent references to the war against the neighbouring countries serve as historical backdrop to events that the novel unfolds. The 1948 Pak invasion on Kashmir, Indo-China war in 1962, Indo-Pak wars during 1965 and 1971 and birth of Bangladesh are some of the events around which the novel rotates.

Similarly, Major Bilimoria's story is successfully woven around pre-Bangladesh war of 1971. His letter to Gustad promulgating that he has joined RAW initiates a wave of rumour, gossip and allegations with Sohrab playing his significant role in it. He alleges that "our wonderful Prime Minister uses RAW like a private police force to do all her dirty work," (93) or to "spy on opposition parties, create troubles, start violence so the police can interfere," or "to treat ballot papers chemically to win election." (93) Bilimoria's alleged role in Mukti Bahini Movement and subsequent implication in an imaginative crime provides another side of the story. Bilimoria's story is fictionalization of a fact, because it is based on the 'Nagarwala Case' of the 1960s. Mistry feels, this story 'waiting to be told' by the side of historiographical account which might have been just peripheral or must have excluded it deliberately to please the centre of power, and centralizes it in his narrative.[9]

Mistry's recent work, *A Fine Balance* is remarkable for its sustained readability and clarity. The design of the story is quite simple. Within its 614 pages lies an account of social and historical developments of a country. With an unnamed city (Mumbai) at the centre, Mistry weaves together a subtle and compelling narrative about four unlikely characters who come together soon after the government declares a 'state of internal emergency.' In the tiny flat of Dina Dalal, Ishvar and Omprakash Darji and Maneck Kohlah are painfully constructing new lives which become entwined in circumstances no one could have foreseen. Mistry prefers to deal with 'adyatan bhoot' (recent past) which is a seminal and phenomenal departure from the tradition. Unlike *Such a Long Journey* which uses imaginary names for real events or persons, *A Fine Balance* gives popular versions of the real events. The physical distance from his motherland gives Mistry a better position to review it.

Mistry has an ability to make his characters articulate his own thoughts or popular versions of the fact. However there is no direct reference to any real, political figures except the scene of the Prime Minister's speech, after declaration of the state of Emergency: "lots of lies have been spread about the Emergency, which had been declared specially for the people's benefit. . . . Wherever the Prime Minister goes, thousands gather from miles around, to see her and hear her. Surely this is the mark of a truly great leader."[11] Mistry is sceptical about the declaration of emergency, it is very natural for him to centralize the exclusions of the historiographers. The chronology of the narration makes it obvious. The book opens with a chapter titled 'Prologue 1975' and ends with 'Epilogue 1984,' after the assassination of the Prime Minister. Even the partition of the subcontinent seems remote, only occasional references are made about it. Mistry normally depicts more than one version of the event/fact he is referring to.

For the common people the Emergency is nothing but 'one more government tamasha' (5): "No consideration for people like us. Murders, suicide, Naxalite-terrorist killing, police custody, death—everything ends up delaying the trains." (6) For Dina it is "government problems—games played by people in power. It does not affect ordinary people like us." (75) However she is proved wrong as it did affect the ordinary people in more than one way. The upper-class people are fascinated by the Emergency. For them it is a magic wand, capable of curing all diseases and decay. The students were euphoric too for a different reason. They felt that by following Jaya Prakash Narayan, they could bring in a change which would "invigorate all society, transform it from a corrupt, moribund creature into a healthy organism." (243) The novel serves as a window of 'human possibility' with particular reference to a 'microscopic' community. It offers a kaleidoscopic view of the emergency. Mistry deals with excesses of emergency at length.

The people like Sergeant Kesar and Thakur Dharmsi had a free hand which soon disenchanted people from 'hi-fi' promises of the government. The beautification drives deprived people of their homes and the forced sterilization camps deprived youth like Om of their dreams. The officers-in-charge of various projects manipulated the figures to their advantage. People were reduced to a community: "Late in the day the truck arrived at an irrigating project where the facilitator unloaded the ninety-six individuals. The project manager counted them before signing the delivery receipt." (331) To add to the woes, the constitution and relevant laws were amended or modified to suit the purpose of the people at the centre. "'What are we to say, madam,' laments Mr. Valmik, 'what are we to think about the state of this nation? When the highest court in the land turns the Prime Minister's guilt into innocence.'" (562) The assassination of the Prime Minister worsens the situation. A taxi-driver advises Maneck to shave off his beard. Homicide and arson paralyzed the city-life. The taxi-driver believes that the Prime Minister deserved her fate, "she gave her blessings to the guns and bombs, and then these wicked, violent instruments began hitting her own government . . . all her chickens came home for roasting." (582)

Mistry's version of history has different dimensions. He focuses on those moments or processes that are produced in the articulation of what Homi Bhabha calls 'cultural differences.' Parsis in *Such a Long Journey* and Chamars in *A Fine Balance* offer social articulation of difference, from the minority perspective. This proliferation of 'alternative histories of the excluded' produces a pluralist anarchy on one hand and recreates the nation it belongs to on the other. The novel gains its effective strength from an interplay of fact and fiction. However, the triumph of Mistry's novel lies in the fact, to borrow Ashley Myles' term, "that it serves as a window of 'human possibility' with particular reference to forgotten microscopic community." Through the characters like Gustad, Dinshawji, Bilimoria, Peerbhoy, Dilnavaz and Miss Kutpitia and a happy combination of standard English and 'Parsi language' Mistry has incorporated ancient myths with living condition of Parsis as a community. This has made the novel a social document. The novel emerges as a parallel history of modern India. It is history from a writer's point of view that tries to dis/uncover the suppressed or neglected chapters of Indian history. By re-narration of history, the novelist constructs his story of his community and nation both.

NOTES

1. Raymond Aron, *Introduction to the Philosophy of History* (London: Weidenfeld and Nicolson, 1938), p. 15.
2. Harry Elmer Barnes, *A History of Historical Writing* (New York: Dover, 1963), p. 3.
3. *Ibid.*, p. 19.
4. Hayden White, *The Content of the Form* (London: The John Hopkins Univ. Press, 1987), pp. ix-x.
5. Friedrich Nietzsche, "Beyond Good and Evil," *The Complete Works of Friedrich Nietzsche*, ed. Oscar Leuy (Edinburgh: Edinburgh U.P., 1923), p. 167.
6. Ezra Pound, "Some Recent Directions in American Cultural History," *American Historical Review*, LXXIII, February 1968, p. 200.
7. Hayden White, "Interpretation in History," *New Literary History*, Vol. IV (1972), p. 281.
8. Droysen, qtd. Hayden White, "Interpretation in History," p. 284.
9. Rohinton Mistry, *Such a Long Journey* (London-Boston: Faber and Faber, 1991), p. 306.
10. A.K. Singh "Rohinton Mistry's *Such a Long Journey*: Re-narrating a Country and Community," *Indianization of English Language and Literature*, ed. R.S. Pathak (New Delhi: Bahri, 1994), p. 199.
11. Rohinton Mistry, *A Fine Balance* (New Delhi: Rupa, 1995).
12. Ashley Myles, "Allan Sealy's *The Trotter-Nama*: A Critical Evaluation," *Recent Indian Fiction*, ed. R.S. Pathak (New Delhi: Prestige, 1994), pp. 78-79.

"And everything ends badly" :
A Reading of *A Fine Balance*

VINITA DHONDIYAL BHATNAGAR

R ohinton Mistry's latest novel *A Fine Balance*[1] weaves together a tale of the 1970s India in the midst of a state of Emergency through the lives of its four main characters: Ishvar and Omprakash Darzi, Dina Dalal and Maneck Kohlah. The Emergency intrudes obtrusively into the lives of all of these characters leading to their eventual loss and destruction. Thus Dina Dalal, by the end of the novel has lost her prized independence and had to seek shelter in the patriarchal protection of her elder brother, Nusswan. Omprakash is castrated in an act symbolic of the impotency of the general populace of India during the authoritarian regime of Indira Gandhi's Emergency. Ishvar is crippled by the loss of both his legs and is reduced to begging for a living. And Maneck, the boy from the Himalayas, throws himself in front of a moving train in a grotesque parody of the reported death sequence of his friend, Avinash. The overall scenario is grim. If a fine balance must be maintained between hope and despair, the end of the novel forfeits that balance. Why do events move towards this inevitable conclusion and what does the text not say in order to say what it does? This paper will attempt to explore the ways in which this text highlights the elements of despair to the cost of presenting an accurate description of the forces of resistance that finally ensured that the Emergency did not last forever, whether it was individuals who heroically braved punishment, bureaucrats who refused to conform or newspapers who continued to highlight the oppressive nature of the authoritarian rule.

The book begins with a quotation from Balzac's *Le Pere Goriot*:

Holding this book in your hand, sinking back in your soft arm chair, you will say to yourself: perhaps it will amuse me. And after you have read this story of great misfortunes, you will no doubt dine well, blaming the author for your own insensitivity, accusing him of wild exaggeration and flights of fancy. But rest assured: this tragedy is not fiction. All is true.[2]

Mistry sets out to tell the reader the 'truth' about India in the mid-1970s. Who is this reader? What is this truth? The publication of this book by Faber indicates a cosmopolitan readership, one willing to pay near about 16 pounds to read this monumental work. The praise from newspapers such as *The Observer, The Spectator* or *The Sunday Times* points to Mistry's previous success as a novelist. *The Spectator* writes: "A rich, humane work undoubtedly one of the best novels about India in recent years." We do not know whether the writer speaks with an awareness of all the regional literature produced in India over recent years. I suspect not. The obvious limitation of language thus excludes works written in Bengali, Marathi or Gujarati from receiving such high praise or international awards such as the Commonwealth Writers Prize for the Best Book. This is not to deny the obvious artistic merit of his novels. It is merely to draw attention to the importance of the location of the publisher, the choice of the language of the creative text and the potential readership of a novel in the final reception of the text.

The other question that emerges is: can language ever truly capture 'reality'? Or does language 'distort' reality in the process of fictionalizing it?

To answer this query we turn to a reading of Mistry's *A Fine Balance*. The novel begins in 1975 with the accidental meeting of Ishvar, Omprakash and Maneck Kohlah in a train. Within a page or two of the novel's opening we find a dead body lying on the railway tracks, near the level crossing. "A nice, quick way to go" Maneck thought "as long as the train had struck the person squarely." (5) "Emergency has just been declared in the country and the common people have yet to understand the threat to themselves. One man comments: Sounds like one more government tamasha." (5) Ishvar, Omprakash and Maneck head for Dina's home where they will share lives for a while before their lives are irretrievably shattered. The two tailors are hired to enable Dina to earn a living through selling dresses on contract to Au Revoir Export Company. And Maneck is an old schoolfriend's son who will live as a paying guest in her apartment. All this we learn in the prologue itself. A series of temporal shifts mark the narrative. The first chapter recounts the story of Dina Dalal from the age of twelve and the death of her father to the age of forty two and the hiring of the tailors. The second chapter returns to the present and introduces us to the manager of Au Revoir Exports, Mrs. Gupta. Through Mrs. Gupta's approval of Mrs.

Gandhi's actions we are confronted with the complicity of the Indian
business houses with the outrages committed during this period:

> This event alone would have been enough to ensure Mrs.
> Gupta's happiness, but there were more glad tidings; minor irri-
> tants in her life were also being eradicated—the Prime Minister's
> declaration yesterday of the Internal Emergency had incarcerated
> most of the parliamentary opposition, along with thousands of
> trade unionists, students and social workers, "Isn't that good
> news? She sparkled with joy."
> Dina nodded, doubtful. "I thought the court found her guilty of
> cheating in the election."
> "No, no, no!" said Mrs. Gupta. "That is all rubbish, it will be
> appealed."
> Now all those troublemakers who accused her falsely have been
> put in jail.
> No more strikes and morchas and silly disturbances. (73)

Dina's assumption that the Emergency is irrelevant from the point of
view of the common people turns out to be woefully misguided. As she
struggles to eke out a living for herself, events conspire to strip each
character of dignity and humanity. The acrimony that marks the
relationship between Dina and the tailors at the start of the novel
transforms itself during the course of the narrative to mutual respect and
compassion. Ibrahim, the rent collector, who plays multiple roles of spy,
blackmailer deliverer of threats and harasser of tenants carries a folder
with many compartments and pouches to sort out these roles. Ironically
the landlord finally sacks him, ostensibly for wearing out too many
folders, but in truth because he has become a compassionate rent
collector, an oxymoron in motion.

The third chapter again goes back in time to Ishvar and Omprakash's story. In this section we are confronted with caste oppression at
its starkest. Ishvar's father Dukhi violates caste restrictions in attempt-
ing to make his sons into tailors. This shows surprising courage in a
man who has been socialized into accepting his position in the caste hierarchy unquestioningly.

During his childhood years, he mastered a full catalogue of the real
and imaginary crimes a low-caste person could commit, and the corresponding punishments were engraved upon his memory. By the time he
entered his teens, he had acquired all the knowledge he would need to
perceive that invisible line of caste he could never cross, to survive in

the village like his ancestors, with humilation and forbearance as his constant companions. This is a particularly moving section of the novel bringing to life the sordid living conditions of the lower caste Indians living in rural India. Even the upper caste women are not exempt from oppression. We are told that they resented the birth of two sons to Dukhi: "It was hard for them to be resentful—the birth of daughters often brought them beatings from their husbands and their husbands' families. Sometimes they were ordered to discreetly get rid of the newborn. Then they had no choice but to strangle the infant with her swaddling clothes, poison her, or let her starve to death." (99-100)

Through Dukhi's story we are brought to the time of the Independence struggle in India. It is ironic that pledges of fighting against caste injustice were taken then but are still to be redeemed. The speaker who comes to spread the Mahatma's message says:

> What is this disease? you may ask. This disease, brothers and sisters is the notion of untouchability, ravaging us for centuries, denying dignity to our fellow human beings. This disease must be purged from our society, from our hearts, and from our minds. No one is untouchable, for we are all children of the same God. Remember what Gandhiji says, that untouchability poisons Hinduism as a drop of arsenic poisonous milk. (107)

Though well-intentioned, this kind of rhetoric depends upon the good intentions of the upper castes and classes to create a social change that would enable a truly egalitarian society to come into existence. But as history would readily testify, no power group ever willingly abandons power. What was needed perhaps was not a speaker to speak of tolerance to the upper classes but a preacher who preached revolution to the lower castes and classes. Dukhi works towards an individual revolution-breaking with life long traditions—to apprentice his sons as tailors with Ashraf:

> It soon became known in Dukhi's village that his children were learning a trade other than leather working. In the old days, punishment for stepping outside one's caste would have been death. Dukhi was spared his life, but it became a very hard life. He was allowed no more carcasses, and had to travel long distances to find work. Sometimes he obtained to hide secretly from fellow chamars, it would have been difficult for them if they were found out. The items he fashioned from this illicit leather had to be sold

in far off places where they had not heard about him and his sons. (118-19)

In the end of course "everything ends badly." Twenty years pass after independence and nothing changes. Narayan says: "Government passes new laws, says no more untouchability, yet everything is the same. The upper-caste bastards still treat us worse than animals." (142)

Narayan points to the fact that as a chamar he cannot still drink water at the village well, worship in the temples of the upper castes or walk where he likes. When he attempts to assert his right to vote, he is brutally tortured and then hanged in the village square. Other untouchables are beaten up at random, their women raped and their huts burnt down. The Thakur decided that Dukhi's family deserves special punishment: "What the ages had put together, Dukhi had dared to break asunder; he had turned cobblers into tailors, distorting society's timeless balance. Crossing the line of caste had to be punished with the utmost severity." (147)

Dukhi, Roopa, Radha and the daughters along with Narayan's corpse are burnt alive at the behest of the Thakur. Omprakash dreams of revenge but both Ashraf and Ishvar know the futility of such dreams and instead decide to send Om to Bombay. With this move, a new phase starts in the lives of Om and Ishvar. In the city it is class rather than caste that oppresses them. They are forced to stay in jhopadpattis that are mowed down. They are rounded up with the street beggars and forced to work as unpaid labour. Their attempts to live their lives with some semblance of dignity are frustrated at various points. On the other hand they do meet an interesting variety of characters such as the Monkey Man or Rajaram. Though Mistry's tone through this section of the novel is slightly jocular, he does manage to let us see the reality behind the glamour of the Dream city, Bombay.

The fifth section of the novel deals with the story of Maneck. His story is the story of the ecological denudation of the Himalayas through the forces of "development" and the death of indigenous enterprise through the entry of multinationals:

But the day soon came when the mountains began to leave them. It started with roads. Engineers in Sola topis arrived with their sinister instruments and charted their designs on reams of paper. They promised roads that would hum with the swift passage of modern traffic. Roads, wide and heavy-duty, to replace scenic mountain paths too narrow for the broad vision of nation-builders and World Bank officials. (215)

Mr Kohlah's increasing sense of loss colours his relationship with his son who becomes increasingly alienated from his father. Maneck is sent to study air conditioning and refrigeration in Bombay and meets the dynamic student leader, Avinash. Avinash really represents the voice that is silenced by Mistry's narrative. For every display of force there is always a resistance. That resistance was not less heroic in the period of the Emergency than during the course of the freedom struggle. That heroism is not officially documented or publicized but it nevertheless existed. For a brief while we are given a glimpse of that aspect of the Emergency in the portrayal of Avinash:

> The mood was euphoric. The students fervently believed their ex-
> ample would inspire universities across the country to undertake
> radical reforms, which would complement the grassroots move-
> ment of Jaya Prakash Narayan that was rousing the nation with a
> call to· return to Gandhian principles. The changes would invig-
> orate all of society, transform it from a corrupt, moribund creature
> into a healthy organism that would, with its heritage of a rich and
> ancient civilization, and the wisdom of the Vedas and Upanishads,
> awaken the world and lead the way towards enlightenment for all
> humanity. (243)

Mistry describes the brief spell of optimism, the formation of stu-dent bodies, agendas adopted and resolutions passed. But his emphasis is on the experience of Maneck who refuses to get involved in any of such activities and resents the fact that he has lost the company of his friend because of his involvement with such work. Avinash mysteri-ously disappears. Maneck only makes a half-hearted attempt to find him. This mysterious disappearance of Avinash meets the narrative logic of Mistry's novel: that everything ends badly. Avinash seems to have been introduced only to reaffirm this philosophy. But the percep-tive reader is left with an uneasy feeling. If resistance is at all possible then why don't the central characters make it more heroic. Dina suc-cumbs to her fate and ends up as an unpaid and glorified servant of Nus-swan's household. Ishvar and Om return to their native place only to be further humiliated. The only act of defiance is Om's spitting at the Thakur for which he is punished with castration. What happened to his plans of motivating an army of chamars to offer resistance to the op-pressive social practices of the Thakurs? What happened to all the strategies that he had learnt of the Naxalites and other militant groups of the North East. And why does Maneck run away to Dubai and complain of the emptiness of life when he could have filled his life and given meaning to it by mobilizing support against the forces that threatened to destroy his home town. Ultimately *A Fine Balance* is the story of individuals rather than of India. Almost twenty-three years after the events of the novel we find a Dalit government at the helm of affairs at U.P. and the voice of the lower castes becoming increasingly assertive in the mainstream of our political life. The mandalization of Indian society has brought the simmering caste tension to the surface but it did not happen overnight. Obviously there has been an increasing awareness among the lower castes and an increasing ability to become agents rather than mere victims in their own dramas. By refusing to grant his characters this agency and presenting them ever and always merely as victims, Mistry has overlooked some of the facts that constitute Indian reality. Similarly in the light of what we know of the Chipko movement or the Narmada dam project we know that resistance to insensitive governmental policies is possible and success, however partial, can be achieved. Laws in urban areas in Independent India favour the tenants over the landlords, however ineffective these laws may be in practice. All over the country there are groups working for social change—publishing booklets, organizing agitations, working against slum demolitions, promoting literacy, resisting the destruction of mosques in secular India. We do not live in an idyllic world but all over the country there are individuals fighting to make the system more just, humane and sensitive. Mistry de-emphasizes such individuals and their concerns in order to write his novel in a particular way. This should not be seen as a negative judgement of his work. If Mistry's "truth" is incomplete it is because it is in the nature of fiction to be incomplete and self-contradictory. A text presents reality partially or incoherently, leaving gaps. Through these gaps a reader can see what the text was hiding from itself. In the case of Mistry's *A Fine Balance* this gap, this silence, is represented by the vision and the experience of Avinash. By removing him from the scene of action before he can seriously alter the chain of events by influencing Maneck and changing his philosophy, Mistry attempts to prevent any disruption of the narrative flow of his novel. When Avinash reappears—he is dead and no longer disruptive of the narrative logic. He has become yet another victim and the suicide of his three sisters further adds to the pathos. The stage is set for everything to end badly and any voice that could have questioned this statement has been necessarily silenced.

Mistry's novel is an incredible achievement. It makes for compelling reading, rich with detail and with memorable characters. And to a large extent it tells some truths about India—truths that need to be told.

But as this paper has attempted to prove, it does not tell the truth about India. For everything here need not end badly.

NOTES

1.   Rohinton Mistry, *A Fine Balance* (London: Faber and Faber, 1995).
2.   Honore de Balzac, *Le Pere Goriot*, qtd. Mistry, *A Fine Balance*.

Designer Quilt: A Study of *A Fine Balance*

B. INDIRA

> Just keep connecting patiently, Dinabi, that the secret . . . it all
> seems meaningless bits and rags till you piece it together. (403)

In a series of connected events spanning over the pre-independent India to the assassination of Indira Gandhi, Rohinton Mistry attempts to show the vulnerability of the average man's life. The novel, *A Fine Balance*[1] also shows how political changes mercilessly cut through the psycho-social fabric of a country where 'justice is sold to the highest bidder.' Caught in the cross-currents of frenzied political changes, even the simplest wishes of a square meal a day and a wife to carry on the family are shattered. The period of Emergency is as much a blotch on the country's conscience as partition had been, not to think of the riots following the assassination of Indira Gandhi.

Emergency, a defence of an insecure leader, disturbs the coherence of routine of the average lives of Ishvar Darjee and his youthful nephew Omprakash Darjee and their employer Dina Dalal, a middle-aged widow and her paying guest Maneck Kohlah. Dina and Maneck are only the indirect victims of Emergency as their lives are dependent on the lives of the tailors, Ishvar and Om. All of them are aware of something stifling their lives though they cannot link it to the existing political scenario of the country. Their struggle for survival, as far as they are concerned does not have a political angle to it. They all believe that the oft-heard word Emergency is a sort of a game played by the power centre and it would not really affect the ordinary people like them. Hence each in his way tries to connect the pervading discomfort and insecurity to their problems of the here and now. Very soon when their simplest dreams get thwarted they are forced into realizing the mayhem created by the Emergency.

Ishvar Darjee, a chamar by caste and a tailor by profession and his youthful rebellious nephew Om come to the city of Mumbai with the hope of making a little money and returning to their village to start afresh. For Dina Dalal, struggling to stand erect against a brother who feels secure in her dependency on him, the tailors are god-sent. For Maneck, a victim of separation-anxiety, Om is a respite from his pressure of conforming to peoples' expectations. Struggle is the centre of all their lives and everybody is the other's centre.

Once at Dina Dalal's there seems to be a revival of hope in the tailors' lives. As the tailors go on to transform the lengths of cloth according to specified patterns, Dina patiently collects the left over bits and pieces for making a quilt. Maneck remarks:

> "Too many different colours and designs," he said . . . "it's going to be very difficult to match them properly."
> ". . . But that's where taste and skill come in. What to select. What to leave out—and which goes next to which," replies Dina. (273)

And each colour and each design in the quilt has a story to tell that has a direct bearing on Dina.

For Ishvar and Om, the huge cut-outs of the Prime Minister with inspiring slogans for hard work and sincerity are mere markers in the confusing labyrinth of the city streets. However, they realize the implication when they are forcibly bundled away to the Prime Minister's meeting to fill in the numbers. With neither the promised tea nor the free bus raid Ishvar and Om return thirsty and tired. "We could have stitched six dresses. Thirty rupees lost," (207) worries Ishvar. For Dinabai their absence is the usual sign of arrogance of the labour class, once their meal is assured.

The second blow is when the tailors' shack is bulldozed to ground as part of slum evacuation programme. Ishvar is content that at least their sewing machines are safe at Dinabai's. They stuff all their belongings in a trunk and, sinking under its weight, go all over the city in search of a place to live in. They realize that even to sleep on the platform they must pay the policeman. Maneck is put off by Dina aunty's refusal to accommodate even the tailors' trunk. Dina is happy at least now Maneck would not have to honour the tailors' invitation for a dinner.

> They ignored each other for most of the evenings but while working on the quilt after dinner, she spread out the squares. . . .
> "Well Maneck? How does it look now?"

"Looks terrible!" he was not ready to forgive her while the tailors remained unaccommodated in the night. (305)

The third blow of Emergency in their lives is when Ishvar and Om are picked up by the police from their rented footpath dwelling to work as construction workers as part of the city beautification project. Ishvar's protest that they are not street urchins or beggars fall on deaf ears. They are forced into a truck wherein 'Underfoot, stray gravel stabbed the human cargo.' (326) The tailors are forced to abandon their work for a number of days for reasons beyond their control. Maneck tries to pacify the agitated Dina Aunty.

"Ishvar and Om wouldn't stay absent just like that," said Maneck. "Something urgent must have come up."
"Rubbish. What could be so urgent that they cannot take a few minutes to stop by?" replied Aunty. (333)

That night Dina is too disturbed to work on the quilt and the pieces "sit in a pile on the sofa hiding their design." (334) Between the two of them, Maneck and Dina decide to finish the dresses. While both of them are at work, Dina realizes how similar Om and Maneck are. And through Maneck she comes to know the long-drawn suffering of Ishvar and Om, inheritors of caste-victimization. "Compared to theirs, my life is nothing but comfort and happiness. . . . People keep saying God is great, God is just, but I'm not sure." (340)

When the stack of remnants sinks, Dina resorts to all those rejected pieces of chiffons to stitch the quilt. When the chiffons too run out, the quilt ceases to live. Dina begins to empathize with the tailors with Maneck giving voice to her muted sympathy. She offers them her verandah to live in when they return to her in a state of shock. Om and Maneck are delighted to be living under the same roof. Now the quilt breathes life again: "She sat with the patches after dinner, 'These new pieces are completely different in style from the old ones,' remarks Maneck." (403)

The quilt maker has shed several of her defences and pretensions. Very soon she even shares her kitchen with them. And as Ishvar begins to trust her with bits of their past, more pieces are joined to the growing story of the tailors. "Sailing under one flag" and getting busy with the quilt making, days pass by "as comforting and liquid as a piece of chiffon" (185) between one's fingers.

Ishvar's obsession to get his nephew married takes the tailors back to their village. By now the quilt is left with a two square-foot gap at the end. All of them spread to quilt holding the opposite ends. '

"Look." Om pointed, "look at that—the poplin from our first job."

" . . . Hungry stomachs were driving our fingers," chuckled Ishvar.
. . .

" . . . And the chiffon . . . it made Om lose his temper. . . . Our house was destroyed by the Government, the day we started on this cloth."

Finally Ishvar concludes: "Calling one piece sad is meaningless. See, it is connected to a happy piece. . . . That's the rule to remember, the whole quilt is much more important than any single square." (490)

In the absence of the tailors, Dina busies herself with the quilt, "straightening a seam, trimming a patch, adjusting what did not look right to her eyes." (509) Dina hopes to complete the quilt once the tailors come back. She and Maneck decide to gift it to Om on his return with a bride.

The final and fatal blow to their lives is an unwarranted police raid on the market place. Ishvar and Om are forcibly taken to a sterilization camp of the village. "The hospital wore festive look with loudspeakers and banners. It's like a mela—little away from the birth control booth is a man selling potions for impotency and fertility." (524)

People like Thakur Dharamsi thrive there auctioning patients who come to clinics, for unless a Government employee produces two or three cases of sterilization, his salary for the month is held back. Provoked by Om's act of spitting towards him, in an act of vendetta, the Thakur, the villain of their family's ruin, orders another operation on the already sterilized Om—the Thakur has a special interest in the boy who is suffering from the testicular tumour, say the nurses. Ishvar's hope of getting a reverse operation done gets sterilized. "What kind of life. What kind of country is this. Where we cannot come and go as we please," wails Ishvar. (540) Ishvar's feet wounded at the beautification project develop gangrene and his legs get amputated. They return to 'our city' with a little trolley fitted with small wheels for Ishvar and a rope for Om to pull it.

Dina, back at her brother's, covers herself with the unfinished quilt recollecting the events and experiences concealed in the rightly knit patches. However, frightened of thinking aloud of the past, she decides to lock it away: "God is a giant quilt-maker, with an infinite variety of designs. And the quilt is grown so big and confusing, the pattern is impossible to see, the squares and diamonds and triangles don't fit well together anymore, it's all become meaningless. So he has abandoned it," (340) remarks Maneck in one of his conversations with Dina Aunty. The quilt-making God, as expected, abandons all of them. Ishvar, Om and Dina who successfully strike a fine balance both within and without go on to live while Maneck reduces himself to a "fallen corncob across the tracks." As Ishvar Darjee puts it, "stories of suffering are no fun when we are the main characters," (383) and this is the story of all of us.

NOTE

1.   Rohinton Mistry, *A Fine Balance* (Calcutta: Rupa by arrangement with London: Faber and Faber, 1996).

A Critical Appraisal of *A Fine Balance*

NILA SHAH

Rohinton Mistry's *A Fine Balance* does not enjoy as much publicity and media hype as Vikram Seth's *A Suitable Boy* did, in India and abroad, yet it has proved its potential by being nominated to the most coveted Booker Prize. In the heyday of magic realism and everything that comes with post-modernism, it takes courage to go back to the traditional way of novel writing.

Our ancient Sanskrit poetics believed "auchitya" (propriety) to be an essential quality in art, Mistry's language and narrative techniques are essentially right for this purpose.

The design of the story is quite simple. Between its opening chapter, "Prologue: 1975" and the concluding one, "Epilogue: 1995," its 614 pages reveal social as well as historical developments of a country. Though the name of the city in which the novel is set is mentioned nowhere, the readers have neither difficulty nor doubt in identifying the 'city by the sea' as Mumbai. It should be noted that Mistry, Rushdie and V.S. Naipaul like to enter India through Mumbai and not through any other city. With the city at the centre, Mistry weaves together a subtle and compelling narrative about four unlikely characters who come together soon after the government declares a 'state of Internal Emergency.' They are aspiring for different pursuits, their fates bring them together to 'sail under one flag.'

In the tiny flat of Dina Dalal, a beautiful widow in her forties, Ishvar and Omprakash Darji and Maneck Kohlah, a young student are painfully constructing new lives which become entwined in circumstances no one could have foreseen. At first Dina and her tailor Om are apprehensive about each other's concerns. Om tries to spy on Dina in order to find out the export company so that he can directly contact them and get orders. As the novel advances, circumstances conspire to deny them their modest aspirations. They all discover that there are other forces at play larger than their individual self. Each faces irrevocable damages. However despite Maneck's disappointments and death, the concluding pages confirm the author's faith in life.

Mistry's metaphorical unfinished quilt is the central message of the story. Unlike Rushdie's metaphor of perforated sheet in *Midnight's Children* or that of the Persian Rug in Maugham's *Of Human Bondage*, the unfinished quilt does not historicize or philosophise but it stands as an eyewitness of collective human efforts.

Dina collects the little pieces of clothes to make a quilt. The other three join in at a later stage. Every little piece of cloth is linked with memory of some or the other event. Like her quilt, the tailor's chronicle gradually gathers shape.[1] Ishvar, for whom 'regrot is luxury' which he could not afford enjoys locating the oldest piece of fabric, moving chronologically, patch by patch re-constructing the chain of their mishaps and triumphs, till they reached the uncompleted corner." (385)

Like the fabric piece of the quilt, Mistry has narrated and re- narrated stories of country, culture and communities around certain point of time and space. Like Peerbhoy Paanwala's fabulous time-honoured yarns about different events in *Such a Long Journey*, *A Fine Balance* is also not a tragedy, comedy or history but "it possesses a smattering of all these characteristics." (306)

It is significant that the successive generations of the writers have exhibited keen interest in 'adyatan bhoot,' the recent past, than 'paroksh bhoot,' the remote past, which is a seminal and phenomenal departure from the tradition. Mistry tries to postulate his own versions of history.

The novel reflects a total view of socio-cultural implications of contemporary society. The author has attempted to bridge the gap between different social and cultural consciousness.

The title is suggestive in more than one sense. Mr. Valmik advocates his Yeatsian theory: "You cannot draw lines and compartments, . . You have to maintain a fine balance between hope and despair." (231) Towards the fag end of the novel, he exclaims again, "There is always hope—hope enough to balance our despair or we would be lost." (503)

The story unravels every aspect of the reality. The author brings his readers face to face with the dilemma of inter-relationship and broken values. He tries to rediscover the Indian identity by setting his novel in three different backgrounds. Dina Dalal lives in a metropolis; Ishvar and Om belong to village while Maneck is from high altitude. A composite picture of a total India with its passions, hopelessness, strength, weakness and beauty pulsates in the novel.

Ishvar and Om belong to the chamar caste. The narrative is a documentary on chamar's ways of life. Trivial details like how they skin the carcass, eat meat and tan the hide are dealt with great interest, and touching subtlety. For instance, "And as he mastered the skills . . . Dukhi's own skin became impregnated with the odour that was part of his father's smell." (98) The novel highlights the specific rural phenomena of frustration and exploitation.

On the other hand, a quiet and content life of a hill station has its own problems. Advent of multinational companies threatens hitherto undisturbed life. Indigenous is juxtaposed with modernization fit. Farokh Kohlah's soft-drink business suffers a heavy setback because of a modernized plant, leading him to reveries.

Besides narrating the living experience, the writer has depicted concerns for the neglected regions of this vast country. It is quite significant as India still lives in villages. Mistry has delineated both, simplicity of rural life and complexities of city life. The shift is remarkably towards an urban and modern situation. In this sense he, like many other Indian writers, is rediscovering his roots and is trying to understand Indian reality in terms of his past experience and tradition.

Mistry's work is not humor. For instance, the hostel rules state, "Please do not bring female visitors of the opposite sex into rooms." (225) The account of the Prime Minister's meeting and Shankar's life-story are just hilarious. The character of Vasantrao Valmik has a Dickensian quality. Ishvar's readymade formula of optimism, "The human face has limited space . . . if you fill your face with laughing, there will be no room for crying" is very crucial to the theme and the title itself.

Towards the end Maneck chooses to end his life while Ishvar and Om continue to try to balance their hope and despair.

Mistry, perhaps oversights the problem of language. It is unlikely that Maneck, a student from North India, the chamars-turned-tailor duo from remote rural area and a Parsi lady of Mumbai can share the same language as India is a multi-lingual country. Moreover, besides some minor flaws or details like chapatis being baked or the villagers using toothbrushes, the readers, especially the non-Gujaratis may be puzzled with the words like 'bhung,' 'Vasnu,' 'Kanasori' just to list a few. Om's frequent use of the expression 'Yaar' even while addressing his uncle sounds strange and a bit out of place.

On the whole, besides some minor quibbles of details, the novel gives a broader dimension to the present-day realities and earns cultural confidence. There is little doubt that Mistry has depicted awareness of his inheritance and complexities of modern life with expertise and vision.

NOTES

1. Rohinton Mistry, *A Fine Balance* (New Delhi: Rupa, 1996), p. 385
2. Rohinton Mistry, *Such a Long Journey* (London: Faber and Faber, 1991).

The Text(ure) of Cruelty: Power and Violence in *A Fine Balance*

PRAMOD K. NAYAR

> A bird came down the Walk—
> He did not know I saw
> He bit an Angleworm in halves
> And ate the fellow, raw.
>
> Emily Dickinson

Rohinton Mistry's *A Fine Balance*[1] is a study of human relationships in a world permeated by and predicated upon cruelty and abused power. Reading Mistry's powerful second novel, one is swiftly alerted to the violence haunting the lives of its characters.

This essay concerns itself with the problematic of power in the novel. The focus is on the display of various forms of power and violence in the novel. The first part of the essay deals with the kinds of power locatable in *A Fine Balance*. The second half reads instances of violence in the text.

I

An undercurrent of violence—potential or actual—runs throughout Mistry's novel. In all cases, violence is related to power relations, and Mistry's novel is no exception.

Power in *A Fine Balance* is mainly of five types: exploitative, manipulative, competitive, nutrient and integrative.[2] These categories are, of course, seldom clearly distinguishable. More often, they modulate into each other, as we shall see in the course of the essay.

Exploitative power is the most prevalent type in the novel. This form of power is always associated with force in *A Fine Balance*. The potential of violence is inseparable from exploitative power. The sway of the upper caste Thakurs in Dukhi's village is a good example. The Thakurs indulge in a perennial caste war against the "Untouchables" of the village. This stranglehold is achieved through recurrent violence—beatings, torture, rape etc. The killing of Narayan is notable for the raw savagery (170-80) of their power.

The Monkey Man likewise tortures his animals, the two monkeys Laila-Majnoo and the dog Tikka. The wretched animals perform antics to entertain people under the perpetual threat of beatings from their master. Later, after the death of the animals the Monkey Man substitutes two children, thus extending cruelty into the human dimension.

The Beggar Master, a Fagin-like character, leads a team of mutilated beggars. They surrender their earnings to him. The Beggar Master's cruelty is also well known. We are informed by the Monkey Man that Beggar Master may have mutilated them to enhance their potential as beggars. (681)

The landlord who harasses Dina Dalal never appears in person. His power is embodied in the thugs and a rent collector who terrorise the tenants. Their power manifests as violence when they beat up Ishvar, Omprakash and Maneck, and vandalise Dina's flat. (524-27)

The Beggar Master offers protection to Dina. Paradoxically, his protection to Dina operates through violence wrought upon others; in this case, the landlord's ruffians. The Beggar Master breaks their fingers and they are thus "persuaded" to leave Dina alone. In return for his protection he has to be paid. Dina and the tailors make veiled references to their own fate if their "protector" is not paid on time. (534-35, 543-45)

If exploitative power hinges upon violence, it is also inextricably linked to profits for the exploiter. The threat of force is used to enhance their own advantage. The Thakurs, for example, obtain cheap labour from the lower caste villagers. When the workers demand their due wages, they are threatened with violence. (127-28) The Monkey Man earns his living by his animals. The Beggar Master's income accrues from the earnings of his beggars. The landlord of course collects the rent from his terrorised tenants.

For exploitative power to be effective, certain choices and decisions have to be made by the power-wielders. To this end, they require a knowledge of prevalent conditions in the terrain where power is to be wielded. Thus an epistemic power[3] precedes the manifestation of exploitative power. For the Thakurs, exploitation follows a thorough understanding of the conditions of the lower castes: their poverty, ignorance and ill health.

A false epistemic base is also established by the exploiters. In the village, the Thakurs connive with the Brahmins for the purpose. They defend their emphasis on purity and caste distinctions as being sanctioned by the scriptures. The "Divine Law" is invoked to reinforce the system. The Brahmin Pandit Lalluram pacifies Dukhi by reiterating the "dharmic duty" of all castes. He enjoins Dukhi to persevere, since the system was required to prevent universal chaos. (137-39) A quiet elision from the literal/verbal to the material/physical has occurred here.

If exploitative power depends on violence manipulative power occurs more covertly. As Rollo May argues, this power is "originally invited by the person's own desperation or anxiety." (107-8) This power is *over* another person. In *A Fine Balance* characters like Nusswan illustrate this power. Nusswan runs the Shroff household after his father's death. From then on, he controls the other members of the family. Dina's young age and their mother's approaching senility make for their total dependence upon Nusswan. He therefore regulates Dina's money, dresses, education and even friendships. Later this power is used to induce Dina into marriage. (34-35) This move however does not work. After a span of time, with widowhood and subsequent penury, she is forced to approach Nusswan for help. Nusswan's monetary assistance helps him retain his hold over her.

Dina herself is not beyond manipulative moves. Ishvar and Omprakash Darji are desperate for jobs. Dina hires them to sew for her, at a meagre wage. She is careful not to give them undue importance, even though they sustain her own existence. Dina does not allow the two to know her suppliers or market. To this end, she seals them, literally, away from the business. She padlocks the front door when she goes to the export house. (98-100)

As may be deduced from the above readings, manipulative power is frequently indistinguishable from exploitative power. The major differentiating factor is the lessened potential of violence in this type of power. It is more sophisticated in its pervasiveness as exemplified by Dina's strategies of using affection and kindness to overcome any resistance from the tailors. The victims almost consent to the manipulation. Most of the time the exploiter uses tactics (coercion, persuasion, emotional blackmail—all seen in Dina's methods) in proportion to the ignorance or lack of ability of the victim. This is demonstrated in Dina's quiet conversion of Omprakash: the pain in his arm→her concern→and medical attention→his gratitude.

A third kind of power is competitive power. This power can also be constructive becauses it produces a healthy rivalry between people, thus improving productivity. Dina Dalal's attempts to squeeze out profits from her small venture are regulated by the constant threat from other similar businessmen. Shankar the mutilated beggar is highly regarded by the Beggar Master because he is the best earner *in comparison to others*.

Government officials in *A Fine Balance* compete with each other to perform more Family Planning operations. Their promotions (over others), salaries and even jobs are at stake. Hence they vie with each other in the programme.

The Kohlah family ruins its business because they do not envisage competition. Maneck's father refuses to compete with rivals regarding it as "absolutely undignified like begging." (269) Here absence of competitive power spells doom.

The fourth category of power Rollo May distinguishes is "nutrient power." This is a power "for" the other, suggestive of a certain care and responsibility. (109) This power generally manifests as paternalism.

In the relationships discussed above, nutrient power is also imbedded alongside other kinds of power. For instance, Dina's brother Nusswan, in spite of his bullying and manipulation, obviously cares for her. He frequently helps her out of difficulty, is concerned for her safety and health, her lonely life and future. In turn, Dina's awareness of her brother's sarcastic tongue and inherent selfishness (Nusswan dismisses the servant each time Dina moves into the house, 58, 702-3) is tempered by her knowledge of his affection.

Dina is not merely an exploitative employer to Ishvar and Omprakash. She is protective and caring on occasions. When Omprakash develops a painful arm, she herself rubs an ointment (386-87) much to the surprise of the two men. Later she allows them to stay in her tiny flat to protect them from police atrocities. When the novel concludes, Dina even risks Nusswan's wrath, feeding the two (now reduced to beggars). She herself wonders how long her conspiratorial good deeds can go on. (750-51)

The Monkey Man adores his pets as his own children. The Beggar Master is actually quite protective towards his "wards," as the handicapped Shankar keeps repeating.

The above illustrations reveal how most of the exploitative powers are also paternalistic. In Mistry, it is the Government which is castigated as undemocratic and unpaternal. Throughout *A Fine Balance*, the Government's exploitative power, cruelty and the evil of juridico-political machinery is emphasised. Herein lies Mistry's savage irony. The Government installed to protect actually robs, maims and kills. The lower level exploiters—individuals—at least temper their exploitative power with gestures of filial affection. Mistry seems to suggest that it is in institutions that exploitations remain "unadulterated," impersonal, and inhuman. Integrative power is the final category that May discusses. Here opposites—thesis and anti-thesis—may come together in a synthesis, in May's terms as "power with the other." (110) In Mistry's novel the synthesis occurs among the marginalised and the exploited. This group forges its own power links. For example, Narayan and two other lower caste villagers rebel against the Thakurs. They oppose them during election time. Dina and the tailors barely manage to keep poverty away by their unity (albeit fragile). They also, in a symbolic instance, ward off peril from the rent collector. (525-27) The doctors are also the exploited, since Government policy forces them into unethical activities through threats. The doctors therefore unite against the victims (of Family Planning) by refusing to take their complaints seriously. (656-57, 660) The victims are themselves integrated against the common oppression.

Mistry's novel is tragic in that this integrative power is never successful in its manifestation. The rebel lower caste villagers are tortured and murdered. The landlord manages to evict Dina. The victims of the forced sterilisation programme do not get justice. Here we reiterate our reading of Mistry: that the system prevents and prohibits validation of any integrative move by individuals. Mistry demonstrates this failure of the system in the character of the Facilitator. These "types" are stooges of the Government, who run their business out of purely personal considerations and with no human feelings. The system thus creates fifth columns within the people to prevent integration. The powers that be remain unaffected, and the result is violence.

II

Potential violence in Mistry's novel traverses certain levels before actualising as violence.

Initially the individuals desire a self affirmation. A great deal of self-consciousness is involved here. Dina's early moves at being "independent" (Dina's favourite theme, as Maneck points out) is an example. The family of the lower caste Dukhi wishes to possess a certain dignity. Maneck, likewise, wants to move from the father's shadow to create a space for himself.

When such attempts at self affirmation meet resistance they become a more overt self-assertion. (40-43) Dina therefore goes and chops off her hair to defy Nusswan. (27) Dukhi takes his children away from the village and trains them in a profession not meant for their caste. Maneck refuses to involve himself in the family business until his father acknowledges his opinions.

Self assertion by the marginalised is inevitably resented by the
dominant powers. This leads, as May demonstrates, to aggression and
violence. Through aggression the individual moves into someone else's
territory. Dina, by living apart rejects Nusswan's hold. Maneck asserts
himself by altering the shop's arrangements. Narayan becomes a tailor
and thus occupies a space allocated to another caste.

All these aggressive moves end in tragedy. Dina loses her independence and returns to Nusswan's charity. The rebel villagers lose their
families and their lives. Maneck commits suicide. Avinash, the student
leader who protests against the Emergency dies due to suspected police
brutality.

Violence, an extension of aggression takes many forms in *A Fine
Balance*. Dina's violence is generally seen in her sarcasm towards
Nusswan. For Dina, this rudeness even while accepting charity from her
brother, is her last attempt at independence. We note her remarks in
Nusswan's office where she has gone to seek his help. (455-56) It sof-
tens the harshness of her helplessness. Maneck, who resents Dina's
motherly advice and restrictions, is often rude. The tailors, especially
Omprakash, smarting about their employee status under Dina are also
rude.

Occasionally violence moves beyond language. There is voyeur-
ism—which violates a person's privacy—which for Omprakash and
Maneck is an attempt to break off, or at least subvert the restraints.
(513-15) Their crude antics and remarks with/about Dina's personal ef-
fects and body (354-56) are also violent acts.

There is an "eco-violence," or violence against nature too. The
Kohlah's village on the mountains loses its pristine beauty in the name
of "beautification" and "progress." The Government uproots people
from their homes in its city-improvement drive. (362-67) This assault is
again Mistry's portrayal of "violence from above."[4]

Maneck's suicide is a violence against his self. However this self-
destructive violence is also an affirmation of his personal ethic and
identity. Maneck returns to find that he has been a "slow coach" left behind. (747) He realises the falsehood of his life, that the dreams and vi-
sions had all failed him. The characters he knew (Dina, Ishvar, Omprakash, Rajaram, even Avinash) had been irrevocably changed. And
with them, his self, treasured by Maneck, had altered too. Maneck's suicide is his final attempt to remain attached to the self he believed he
possessed (the chess set that Avinash gave him, an attachment to their
past, stays with Maneck right upto his death). Thus the self-destructive
violence is a sign of self-affirmation.[5]

Violence in *A Fine Balance* also occurs in the form of positive aggression. Positive aggression occurs when individuals act across barriers and form relationships. (May, 151) This is also, as noted before, a manifestation of integrative power, when, for instance, Dina and the tailors forge a common front, they ignore caste, class, employer/employee barriers. This integration occurs in an aggression against the threat to their existence in the form of the landlord. Another unexpected alliance is that between the tailors and Shankar the beggar. When their life at the project becomes unbearable, the tailors seek Shankar's help to escape. The friendship becomes a dependency. The trio together form a bond to escape an act of transgressive aggression wherein barriers (between them and against them) are broken.

However these bonds of positive aggression are temporal, and the group is anomic. They occur at times of crises and seldom last. This is probably the essential tragedy in *A Fine Balance*. The individuals, however firm they stand, eventually break. The system overwhelms them. The positive stance is always undermined by factors beyond their control.

Mistry is hence depicting courage and simplicity pitted against institutional might. An almost Kafkaesque struggle against the system and its reductive features—exemplified in the mass family planning movement or the slum demolition—occurs in *A Fine Balance*. And ultimately there is failure. If the characters drive a fine balance between "hope and despair" (the terms are always mentioned together in Mistry) circumstances tilt it in favour of despair alone. In Lawrentian terms, Mistry's novel deals with an "essentially tragic age."

NOTES

1. Rohinton Mistry, *A Fine Balance* (London: Faber and Faber, 1996).
2. This categorisation has been adapted from Rollo May's exposition in her seminal work *Power and Innocence: A Search for the Sources of Violence* (New York: Norton, 1972).
3. The term has been used by Peter Morris in *Power: A Philosophical Analysis* (Manchester: Manchester UP, 1972). Similar arguments regarding the equation of knowledge and power have been forwarded by Michael Foucault and Edward W. Said.
4. Rollo May uses the phrase to describe institutional and Governmental violence. She argues that this violence which is a perversion of previous coercive machinery is used for the purpose of warding off threats to the establishment. (186-87)

May's argument is well illustrated in *A Fine Balance* where the Government under the pretext of protection, care, safety actually deprives people of all three. The Family Planning programme, the city beautification drive or irrigation projects are used by Mistry as examples.

5. Maneck's suicide is similar to the self-immolation of Edwina Crane in Paul Scott's *The Raj Quartet* (1966-1975). Crane commits suicide because she realises that the self she believed she had, had failed her. Or rather that it was illusory, an anachronism.

The Politics of Survival and Domination in
A Fine Balance

NOVY KAPADIA

Mistry's novel *A Fine Balance* (1996) is full of vivid images. The crisp verbal pictures do not detract but enhance the overall impact of the free-flowing storyline. The novel begins with the image of a woman at her sewing machine. From that solitary image, the storyline emerges as Mistry explains: "As three more characters [the tailors Ishvar and Omprakash and the Parsi student Maneck] entered the picture, four in all seemed a reasonable number to start with. The next question was where and when to place them. In *Such a Long Journey*, the year is 1971. It seemed to me that 1975, the year of the Emergency, would be the next important year, if one were preparing a list of important dates in Indian history. And so 1975 it was."

The overlapping stories in this novel are neatly inter-woven. Rohinton Mistry uses memory and imagination to depict a turbulent period in Indian history. The author claims that his novels are not 'researched' in the formal sense of the word but that he relies on articles from newspapers, magazines and chats with people from India to collect material. However as Mistry admits, all these details get shaped by his memory and imagination. Though Mistry claims that he is a casual researcher, yet his novel *A Fine Balance* is weighed down by gory details of the horrors of Internal Emergency. All the repercussions and disasters of those totalitarian years like the Kanpur sisters' suicide, castrations, demolitions and sterilisations frequently reappear in this book. Creditably the tone is not the condescension of an expatriate author but Mistry aptly reveals the essential human warmth and dignity that survives in India despite the horrors of Internal Emergency. Commenting on the themes and issues of this novel, the author says, "The way the main characters, the tailors Ishvar and Omprakash, endure suggest that dignity is inherent in the heroic manner in which they strive to survive.

And perhaps in their insuppressible sense of humour." The human endurance of the suffering tailors and others like them who faced the horrors of eviction, sterilisation, forced labour and police brutality is one of the hallmarks of the book. It shows how the underprivileged survive and the author's concern at the plight of the poor and exploited people. The book assumes dimensions of political correctness, as it shows that forces of privilege combine to suppress the lower castes, the rural and urban poor for self-gain.

The book starts with Mistry telling the story through the cynical voice of the student Maneck, sent to study in Bombay. Maneck stays as a boarder at Dinabai, a Parsi widow's house at Bombay. At the same house, the tailors Ishvar and Omprakash, seeking refuge in Bombay due to caste violence in their village, seek employment. So in this way, the lives of Maneck, a Parsi student from a middle-class business family, Dinabai a Parsi widow struggling to make ends meet and preserve her independence from her dominating brother and two lower caste tailors Ishvar and Omprakash get inter-connected. Thus these characters from different class backgrounds start inter-acting with each other and the coincidence does not seem incongruous. So the novel progresses through a series of seemingly separate stories, Dinabai's childhood, romance, early marriage and death of her husband and struggle for survival, Maneck's alienation from his stiff upper lip middle class parents, hassles of college life in Bombay and attempts to forge a human relationship with Dinabai and the struggling tailors Ishvar and Omprakash and above all the caste violence which drove the lower caste tailors from their village to seek employment in the teeming metropolis, Bombay. Coincidence and overlapping stories help to create an intricate plot. The four main characters of this novel suffer from a sense of rootlessness. Oppressive caste violence has driven Ishvar and Omprakash from their traditional occupation (working with leather) to learn the skills of tailoring and from a rural background to overcrowded Bombay. Similarly Maneck moves from the invigorating atmosphere of his home in the hills to Bombay for higher education. Dina has grown up in Bombay but her sense of independence after her husband's accidental death keeps her away from her family. So in a sense all the four main characters are lonely and struggling for identity and survival. Social circumstances, loneliness and a sense of rootlessness bring them together and forge a bond of understanding as they struggle to survive. The human spirit displayed by these four characters of different class backgrounds and ages, despite repeated setbacks upholds Mistry's subtle political theme of how human beings can endure and survive with some dignity despite

oppressive circumstances. Ultimately the four main characters are struggling to maintain 'a fine balance' in their lives.

The novel starts on a note of coincidence. Maneck and the two tailors are sitting in the same compartment of a local train, travelling to the
same destination, Dina's house. As is typical in Indian trains, they start
conversing and realise they are in search of the same address. Initially
both Ishvar and Omprakash are apprehensive that Maneck is a rival for
the job. However they become friendly once they realise that Maneck is
not seeking employment with Dina. Ishvar, the uncle is initially deferen-
tial to Maneck because of the later's class background. However Omprakash who is more independent does not suffer from an inferiority
complex and soon befriends Maneck. The months they spend in Dina's
house helps this friendship bloom and grow. The plight and sufferings
of Omprakash gives Maneck a wider perspective of life and human suffering. Remaining cheerful and retaining a sense of humour despite ex-
cessive adversity are admirable qualities in both Ishvar and Omprakash.
Maneck also benefits by participating in Dina's struggle to retain her
sense of independence. The travails of Ishvar, Omprakash and Dinabai
make Maneck realise that his own problems of alienation from his father
and lack of adjustment with his mates in college are trivial comparison.
The sense of camaraderie that develops as this quartet struggle to meet
the export order deadlines (Dinabai earns her income by providing tai-
lored clothes to an export firm) gives Maneck a more mature attitude to
life. The trials, the tribulations, the shared jokes, intimacies, eating the
same food and sense of adventure enables Maneck realise that life is
often "a fine balance" between happiness and despair. The author implies that at various levels of existence, there is a see-saw struggle between happiness and despair. Life never seems to follow a placid course
in Rohintion Mistry's novels, *Such a Long Journey* and *A Fine Balance*.
There are always upheavals, whether at the slums where Ishvar and Omprakash reside in Bombay or problems of food and political disturbance
at the residential block at Maneck's college, amongst the beggars in the
streets or the emergence of competition which shatters Maneck's father's monopoly of the Cola drinks in his hometown.

Some of these upheavals, like the emergence of competition in the
cold drinks business, occur as part of life's struggle. However, in *A Fine
Balance*, most upheavals take place because of the imposition of internal Emergency. The eviction of the poor from the cities, the forced labour camps, the sterilisations are all manifestations of the Internal
Emergency. During the course of the pulsating narrative, without any
obvious authorial intrusions, Mistry sharply criticises the Internal Emer-

gency. He shows that all the avowed promises of the Emergency to abolish bonded labour, child labour, sati, dowry system, child marriage and harassment of backward castes by upper castes never materialised. Instead as Mistry shows in several instances in the novel a nexus emerges between the police and the established hierarchy either the upper dominance in the villages or the land/building mafia in Bombay.

Various episodes in the novel reveal Mistry's sympathy for the oppressed and concern at authoritarian, oppressive practices during the two year period of Internal Emergency. During the course of the narrative, Mistry makes some revealing political insights. The transition in rural life, the change in aspirations of the lower castes, the attempts by the upper castes to preserve the old order is aptly delineated. A major instance is the violence perpetuated by Thakur Dharamsi and his henchmen against Narayan's family during the week of parliamentary elections. The generation gap is shown in the aspiration of the lower castes. Narayan's father tells his son, "You changed from Chamar to tailor. Be satisfied with that." (143) However Narayan who is educated wants to exercise his rights. He wants to actually vote in the elections and not let the "blank ballots be filled by the landlords' men." (144) Mistry in succinct prose shows the cynical manipulation of elections in rural India.

> On election day the eligible voters in the village lined up outside the polling station. As usual Thakur Dharamsi took charge of the voting process. His system, with support of the other landlords, had been working flawlessly for years.
>
> The election officer was presented with gifts and led away to enjoy the day with food and drink. The doors opened and the voters filed through. . . . They [the lower caste villagers] placed their thumb prints on the register to say they had voted, and departed. Then the blank ballots were filled in by the landlords' men. The election officer returned at closing time to supervise the removal of ballot boxes to the counting stations, and to testify that voting had proceeded in a fair and democratic manner. (143-44)

Two years later when elections take place, Narayan tries to assert his democratic right and cast his own vote instead of abetting the process of rigged elections. For his defiance, Narayan and two other 'Chamars' are forcibly gagged, flogged and tortured. "Burning coals were held to the three men's genitals, then stuffed into their mouths." (146) Finally in terse prose, Mistry describes, "the ropes were transferred from their ankles to their necks and the three were hanged. The bodies were displayed in the village square." (146) Not content with such revenge, Thakur Dharamsi unleashes mayhem by his 'Goondas' in order to teach "those achhoot jatis a lesson." (146) Narayan's family for defying the existing social order pays an extreme price. Dukhi (Narayan and Ishvar's father), Roopa, Radha and the daughters are bound and burnt alive. Mistry implies that the needless arrogance of the upper castes in trying to maintain social supremacy led to the consolidation and emergence of the Dalits in Indian politics. The rise of the Dalits as a political and social force in the 1990s in India and the caste warfare in the countryside, is hinted at by the novelist, Omprakash's contempt and defiance of Thakur Dharamsi on their return to the small town near their ancestral village. Mistry's novel makes an astute political comment because it shows that in rural India, the upper castes aggravated social tensions by their insensitive and churlish behaviour.

The ultimate indictment of the Internal Emergency comes in the description of the 'Nusbandi Mela' in the closing chapters of the novel. The author aptly describes the callous indifference of the authorities who are more keen on "targets have to be achieved within the budget" (533) rather than human welfare, the upliftment of the poor. The author lucidly shows the involvement of an entrenched, insensitive bureaucracy in the demolitions of 'jhuggi-jhopris,' forced labour camps and sterilisation drives. Senior administrators from the Family Planning Centre admonish doctors for not achieving targets. Operations are conducted with partially sterile equipment due to the harsh reprimands of bureaucrats who are only interested in targets and not human suffering. The euphemism of 'efficiency' and 'sense of duty' is used to ensure that sterilisation operations are performed even under unhygenic conditions. The doctors are afraid that "they would be reported to higher authorities for lack of cooperation, promotions would be denied, salaries forzen." (533)

Very cleverly the author shows that vested interests combined with the bureaucracy to perpetuate the status quo under the guise of saving the nation from population explosion. Thakur Dharamsi, the upper caste ring leader, achieves respectability as a political leader during emergency because he organises many sterilisation camps. He uses his superior position to see that Omprakash is castrated, the testacles are removed. In this way Thakur Dharamsi takes revenge on the lower castes in his village whose only crime was to achieve some social mobility by getting educated and sending their children to be trained as tailors instead of working with leather, their traditional occupation. Thakur Dharamsi's cruel misuse of authority shows that the trend of criminalisation of politics and the politicisation of crime, so rampant in India in the last decade of the twentieth century, started in the period of Internal Emergency. This is an astute political insight by the author. Mistry also hints in his novel that constant oppression by the upper castes would lead to violence and an uprising by the lower castes. When Ishvar goes to register a complaint at the police chowki about his nephew's castration, the constable on duty is perturbed: "He wondered if this meant a fresh outbreak of inter-caste disturbances, and headaches for his colleagues and himself." (539) So in a way, Mistry is being quite clairvoyant and hints at the rise of the numerous Dalit Senas in several states in India, as a retaliation against upper caste oppression.

A perusal of the caste background of the members elected to the Lok Sabha in the last four decades will reveal the changing political scenario of India. For instance in the 1st General Elections in 1952, there were 15 Brahmins out of the 48 Members of Parliament elected from Maharashtra. In the 11th Lok Sabha election in 1996, there were no Brahmins amongst the 48 elected from Maharashtra. Including the Reserved seats, there are now about over 200 members of the 11th Lok Sabha, who belong to either Scheduled Castes/Scheduled Tribes or the Other Backward Caste categories. Mistry is well aware of this political change in India. As a sensitive novelist he tries to highlight the reasons for this change. Mistry aptly shows that the callous behaviour of upper caste landlords like Thakur Dharamsi has led to the Other Backward Castes getting united and asserting their political and social rights. The rise of the Bahujan Samaj Party (BSP) formed in 1979 which won 67 of the 428 U.P. Assembly seats and formed the Government along with the Bharatiya Janta Party (BJP) in India's most populous state is an indication of the rise of the Dalits. The social tensions in the villages, the changing aspirations of the lower castes and caste based violence, is so well delineated, so well woven into the flow of the narrative that it makes Rohinton Mistry a very astute political novelist.

M.K. Naik in his learned article "The Political Novel in Indian Writing in English" defines this genre as a novel which either has a strong ideological leaning or one which depicts political events. So by traditional definitions, political novels explain how politics works in particular societies. The finest examples of such writing of course are the works of Aleksandr Solzhenitsyn, whose penetrative works made it impossible for the West to ignore any longer the true nature of the Soviet regime. David Remnick, Moscow correspondent for the *Washington Post* from 1988 to 1992, wrote a memorable book *Lenin's Tomb*, winner of the 1994 Pulitzer Prize for General Non-Fiction. In this book, talking about the impact of Solzhenitsyn's works, David Remnick states, "If literature has ever changed the world, his books surely have. *One Day in the Life of Ivan Denisovich* opened the world of the camps up to the people of the Soviet Union in the early sixties, and the three volumes of *The Gulag Archipelago* erased all lingering doubts in the seventies." (540)

Similarly Charles Dickens delineated the history and the politics of the French Revolution in his magnificent novel, *A Tale of Two Cities*, with a panoramic background representing the dramatic life of a few individuals interwoven with the interest of a major public event. Other great historical-political novels of the twentieth century are Margaret Mitchell's *Gone with the Wind*, a serious evocation of the American Civil War, and Leo Tolstoy's *War and Peace* which describes Napolean's invasion of Russia in Indian English fiction books like Khushwant Singh's *Train to Pakistan* (1956), Manohar Malgonkar's *A Bend in the Ganges* (1964), Attia Hosain's *Sunlight on a Broken Column* (1961) and Chaman Nahal's *Azadi* (1975) all deal with the historical event of Partition and its political ramifications. The respective authors have transmuted facts of history into significant works of art. Rohinton Mistry also belongs to this category. The horrors and traumas of Emergency, the prevalent tensions between the upper and lower castes in rural India, the seething anger of the oppressed and the upsurge of the Dalits are deftly chronicled and presented by Mistry in his epic novel *A Fine Balance* (1996). The ideological concerns of Mistry make him one of the foremost Indian English political novelists of the 1990s.

The ending of the novel is startling and unconventional. Maneck, the brooding Parsi youngman, is upset at the alienation from his family. His sorrows increase,' when he visits Mumbai and finds that Dina has been evicted from her house, has lost her struggle for independence and now stays with her brother. Walking away from Dina's house, he is further perturbed at seeing Ishvar and Omprakash handicapped and working as beggars. The culmination of these series of staggering events is that it drives him to extreme despair and he commits suicide by throwing himself in front of a train. This extreme act has been criticised for making the novel very morbid. However, it is Mistry's way of showing how a member of the privileged middle class, the sensitive Maneck, lost out in the struggle to maintain 'a fine balance between hope and despair.' Rohinton Mistry emerges as the foremost Parsi political novelist for his consistent depiction of ideology and politics in his novels. In other Parsi novels, reference to political events is rare. In *Ice-Candy Man* and *The Crow Eaters* by Bapsi Sidhwa and Dina Mehta's *And*

Some Take a Lover, the ideological stance and contrasting opinions of the Parsi Community to the Freedom Struggle and Quit India Movement are aptly delineated.

Bibliography

Howe, Irving. *The Idea of the Political Novel* (New York: Fawcett, 1967).

Gokhale, Veena. "How memory lives and dies," *The Times of India*, 27 October 1996, Sunday Magazine section.

"A cosmic sick joke: Booker panel rubbishes Mistry novel," *Asian Age*, 31 October 1996, 1.

Mehta, Dina. *And Some Take a Lover*. Delhi: Rupa, 1992.

Mistry, Rohinton. *A Fine Balance*. New Delhi: Rupa, 1996.

Remnick, David. *Lenin's Tomb*. London: Penguin Books, 1994.

Sidhwa, Bapsi. *Ice-Candy Man*. London: William Heinemann, 1988.

_____. *The Crow Eaters*. Delhi: Sangam, 1980.

Index

Anand, Mulk Raj 29, 90
And Some Take a Lover 134
Arnold, Matthew 62
Atwood, Margaret 61, 65n
"Auspicious Occasion" 26, 54, 55-56, 59
Azadi 133

Balzac 102, 109n
Bend in the Ganges, A 133
Bissoondath, Neil 15, 37
Blaise, Clark 14, 15
Bombay Duck 93
Brackley and the Bed 57
Bronte, Charlotte 47

Change of Skies, A 43
Chatterjee, Upamanyu 9, 29
Crow Eaters, The 38-39, 93, 133, 134n

Dabydeen, David 30n
Days and Nights in Calcutta 14
Desai, Boman 30n, 44, 45-47, 53n
Dhondy, Farrukh 30n, 93
Dickens, Charles 133
Digging up the Mountains 15-16
Doctor Zhivago 17

Eliot, T.S. 27, 71, 85, 86, 92n

Faulkner, William 133
Fine Balance, A 9, 17, 19-21, 37, 40-42, 70, 96, 97, 99-134
Firdausi 84

Ghosh, Amitav 9
"Ghost of Firozsha Baag," The 54, 56, 57-58, 59
Gitanjali 28, 31n, 66, 84

Gone with the Wind 133
Gooneratne, Yasmine 38, 42, 43
Grass, Guntur 66
Gulag Archipelago, The 133
Gunny Sack, The 12, 93

Hardy, Thomas 87, 91
Heaven on Wheels 37
Hitopadesha 19
Hosain, Attia 133

Ice Bangles 16
Ice-Candy Man 39-40, 44, 47-50, 53n, 133, 134n
Imaginary Homelands 23, 31n, 69

Jasmine 14
"Journey of the Magi" 27, 71, 85, 86

Kanga, Firdaus 32-37, 93
Katha Sarit Sagar 19
Kesavan, Mukul 9

"Lend Me Your Light" 27, 66-69
Lenin's Tomb 132, 134n

Malgonkar, Manohar 133
"Management of Grief," The 15, 62, 64-65
Maugham, Somerset 116
Mehta, Dina 30n, 133, 134n
Memory of Elephants, The 44, 45-47, 53n
Middleman and Other Stories, The 15, 27n
Midnight's Children 9, 29, 116
Mitchell, Margaret 133
Mrs. Dalloway 81
Mukherjee, Bharati 13, 14, 22n, 30n, 61-65

Nahal, Chaman 133
Naipaul, V.S. 15, 17, 30n, 115
Nietzsche, Friedrich 96, 101n
No New Land 93

Of Human Bondage 116
"Of White Hairs and Cricket" 54,
    56
Ondaatje, Michael 29
*One Day in the Life of Ivan
    Denisovitch* 133
"One Sunday" 54, 56, 59

Pakistani Bride, The 39, 40, 93
Panchatantra 19
Pasternak, Boris 17
Pleasures of Conquest, The 42-43

Raj Quartet, The 126n
Remnick, David 132, 133, 134n
Rushdie, Salman 9, 23, 25, 29, 30n,
    31n, 66, 69n, 115, 116

Sadiq, Nazneen 16
Sartre, Jean-Paul 66-69
Scott, Paul 126n
Sealy, Allan 101n
Selling Illusions 37
Seth, Vikram 9, 19, 115
Shah-Nama 27, 84
Shakespeare, William 87, 91
Sidhwa, Bapsi 29, 38-40, 44, 47-50,

    53n, 93, 133, 134n
Singh, Khushwant 90, 133
Solzhenitsyn 132, 133
Sound and the Fury, The 133
"Squatter" 62-64
Such a Long Journey 9, 17-19,
    20-21, 25, 27-30, 31n, 32-37,
    44, 50-52, 53n, 70-95, 96,
    97-99, 100, 101n, 116, 118n,
    127, 129
Suitable Boy, A 19, 115
Sunlight on a Broken Column 133
"Swimming Lessons" 27, 54, 58-59,
    60

Tagore, R.N. 28, 31n, 66, 67, 84
Tale of Two Cities, A 133
Tales from Firozsha Baag 9, 16, 25,
    31n, 37, 54-69, 70
Tharoor, Shashi 9
Tolstoy, Leo 133
Train to Pakistan 133
Trotter-Nama, The 101n
Trying to Grow 32-37, 93

Untouchable 20

Vassanji, M.G. 12, 93
War and Peace 133

Wife 14
"Wife's Story," A 15